# SQUARE PEG

## Memoirs of a Misfit Miner

Also by Gordon Ottewell

Journey from Darkness (children's story)
Family Walks in South Derbyshire
A Cotswold Country Diary
Discovering Cotswold Villages
Gloucestershire Countryside
Literary Strolls in the Cotswolds & Forest of Dean
Literary Strolls in Wiltshire & Somerset
The Evenlode: An Exploration of a Cotswold River
Tangleton (children's story)

Barn Owl Books
33 Delavale Road, Winchcombe, Cheltenham,
Gloucestershire, GL54 5YL, United Kingdom
☎ 01242 603464

First Published 2008

ISBN 978-0-9510586-7-1

Typeset by Limited Edition Press
Printed through SS-Media Ltd.

British Library Cataloguing in Publication Data.
A catalogue record for this book is available
from the British Library.

Cover by Geoff Maynard
With special thanks to Robert Talbot for his invaluable help.

# SQUARE PEG

## MEMOIRS OF A MISFIT MINER

*Gordon Ottewell*

## GORDON OTTEWELL

**Barn Owl Books**

The Author, 1956

# Chapter 1

**M**y letter of application, over which I had laboured for so long, disappeared into the postbox and with a heavy heart I turned for home. Opening the kitchen door I could see at a glance that nothing had changed. My parents were still seated at the kitchen table, just as I had left them. The pen, ink bottle and writing pad bore testimony to my recent reluctant efforts. The atmosphere remained tense. Father looked up.

'You've posted it, then?'

I nodded. 'Good. They'll get it tomorrow. With a bit of luck you'll get called for interview next week.'

Mother gave one of her long-suffering sighs. 'I never thought I'd live to see the day when a son of mine would be a collier.'

It was the early summer of 1947. I was sixteen and had just applied for the post of trainee on the surveying staff of the local group of collieries. Like all the other pits scattered along the Derbyshire-Nottinghamshire border, these had on the first day of that year been taken over by the National Coal Board.

My father, at whose insistence I had applied for the post, squirmed uncomfortably.

'He's not going to be a collier, Mother', he said in his best placatory voice. 'It's an office job - surveying, drawing plans, using figures. It's his chance to make a career for himself. It's not pit work – it's draughtsmanship. You'll see.'

My mother looked far from convinced. 'But you said yourself that he might have to go down the pit sometimes,' she persisted, eyeing me with the anxious frown that my presence always seemed to induce. 'If that's not being a collier, I don't know what is. Worries me sick to think about it.'

Cornered, my father glowered at me dangerously. 'We've been through this often enough before,' he pronounced heavily. 'He should have made the best of his chances at school, instead of wasting his time scribbling and bothering about cricket and -.' His words tailed off, as though to spare her a complete catalogue of my transgressions. United in the face of adversity, they gazed at the source of their concern with sad bewilderment.

'I don't know, I'm sure I don't,' my mother lamented, nodding helplessly.

'We've done all we can, Mother,' my father, as so often before, assured her. 'Paid through the nose to give him the best education money can buy, and what do we get?' His fist thumped down on the kitchen table. 'We've done enough - it's up to him now.'

**\*\*\*\*\*\*\*\*\*\*\*\*\*\*\*\*\***

Surrounded as we were by pits, I knew appallingly little about them, or about the men who worked in their hidden depths. My father was a self-employed joiner and builder. There were no pitmen either in his or in my mother's family. We lived in one of a straggle of 1920s houses climbing the slope above the nearest colliery, the homes of families generally considered - in their own eyes at least - as somewhat superior to the mining folk comprising the majority of the population of the nearby village.

Inwardly I acknowledged the truth of my father's remarks about my lack of achievement at school. Six years earlier, the headmaster of the village school had prepared him for the fact that I was by no means certain of obtaining a scholarship to the grammar school. My arithmetic was weak and there were several candidates, most of them pitmens' children, jostling for position to snap up the few available places. Father was thunderstruck. The fact that I was said to have a certain aptitude in English, history and nature study was of no consolation. His son, his only child, born after twelve years of marriage and indulged with every advantage that money could buy, yet a duffer at arithmetic and unlikely to win a place at grammar school - it was unthinkable.

Father, however, was a fighter, a man of action; meek acceptance of fate's cruel blows was utterly foreign to his

6

nature. No son of his would suffer the humiliation of failure - not if he could help it. He heard of a small private school in a nearby town, a cramming establishment staffed exclusively by women, with something of a reputation for getting grammar-school rejects up to School Certificate standard on a forcibly-fed diet of academic stodge. The fees were high and money, in the early years of the war, in short supply. But father did not flinch; what his son lacked, he would pay for, whatever the cost.

I emerged from these six stultifying years with the unremarkable haul of two credits and five passes - scant reward for all the sacrifices made on my behalf. My ambitions, such as they were, were twofold - to play for my county and country at cricket and to write books on the game. I was unsure of the order of preference and entertained the secret hope of fulfilling both ambitions simultaneously.

My one distinction at school - not that it could truthfully be called a distinction - was to have been caught during an interminably arid maths lesson writing a series of paragraphs on the cricketing prowess of certain of my classmates, as revealed in the knockabout games we were grudgingly allowed to play at lunchtime. The teacher who caught me in the act stared at my literary efforts in speechless incomprehension and sent me to the headmistress, who after summarily glancing at the offending pages, .handed them back with the suggestion that my time, and my parents' money, would be better spent if I gave my undivided attention to my schoolwork.

The crowning blow to my father had been my failure to obtain a pass in mathematics. He was angry, perplexed and bitter. He had sat with me for hours, watching with mounting frustration my utter ineptitude at the subject. Fuming, he had snatched the pen from my hand and demonstrated the errors of my ways. He had filled countless pages with explanatory diagrams and alternative methods of working. Eager to detect some modest sign of improvement, he had been quick to lavish praise at any slight hint of enlightenment, only to explode in exasperation later when these hopes were proved false.

We spent hours that summer deliberating what was to be done. I had left school unqualified and unsung. Too late, it seemed, I began to experience a certain vague uneasiness about the future; England's fortunes in the Tests against South Africa and the county's struggles in the lower reaches of the championship table were for once banished from the forefront of my mind as I grappled with this totally new and unanticipated state of affairs.

'What do you *want* to do?' Father asked again and again in desperation. I tried unsuccessfully to come up with something that would link my fantasies, however tenuously, with the world of his experience.

'I wouldn't mind being a journalist,' I proffered. The ensuing silence was heavy with foreboding.

'What - writing - on a paper?' Father's incredulity could hardly have been greater had I suggested being a pirate.

'But - that would mean London, wouldn't it? 'Mother interjected. I pointed out that a thriving evening paper was published in the county town. Father took advantage of the respite to gather his thoughts.

'Nothing but an office boy!' he scoffed. 'Making tea and going to funerals. Besides, it wouldn't pay your bus fare.'

'But I *like* writing,' I reasoned. 'It's the only thing I want to do. Besides, it's the only thing I can do, come to that.' Father, however, would have none of it. .

'You can get nowhere without maths,' he declared emphatically, touching yet again a raw nerve. Heatedly, I reminded him that the boy next door, who had no academic qualifications whatever, had recently had a successful audition with a nationally famous symphony orchestra. This was the last straw.

'Musicians? Umph – ten a penny!' Father snorted. 'Call that a career? End up on the dole, he will. You mark my words.'

*****************

A week or so after submitting my letter of application, I was called over to the area headquarters of the newly-formed National Coal Board, about five miles away, with instructions to ask for the office of the Area Chief Surveyor. This somewhat dilapidated office block stood on the edge of a typically stark pit village overlooking the largest colliery in the area. Rows of mean-looking houses lay in geometric order within a stone's throw of the pithead, each with its grubby little garden of soot-black soil, at the foot of which stood an earth closet surmounted by a high brick wall.

My languishing spirits rose somewhat when on reaching an upstairs landing, I discovered that a cricket field lay just across the road........Two or three seasons here, then on to the county ground staff ........First class debut at twenty-one, say...........

Opening a door, I found myself in a large low-ceilinged room illuminated by long strip lights. Beneath these, several men were bending in deep concentration over immense wooden tables, upon which large sheets of brightly-painted linen were draped, held down at the corners by leather-covered weights. I was told that as 'The Chief' was not yet ready to see me, I was free to look around until I was called for.

Diffidently picking my way between the tables, I noticed a slightly-built man with a pallid, deeply-wrinkled face seated alone at a small table in a corner of the room. He seemed to be examining the pen in his hand with rapt attention. Uneasily conscious of the looks of curiosity of the younger men, I hovered in the vicinity of this fatherly-looking figure, who as yet appeared unaware of my presence. I could now see that the coloured sheets were in fact plans of underground workings, drawn and coloured with considerable care and skill. The man had been engaged in printing the title lettering on one particular plan and the artistry he displayed caused me to pull up in silent admiration. So this was draughtsmanship. I was impressed.

At length the man spoke. The words, few in number, were delivered downwards from an invisible mouth located somewhere between the wrinkles of the partly-hidden face. Was he addressing me? Still he did not look up.

'I ......I beg your pardon?' I said.

Suddenly he wheeled round, flinging the pen across the room, accompanying the action with a frenzied outpouring of every wicked and secret obscenity I had ever heard, as well as several entirely and intriguingly new to me. I stood rooted to the spot, uncomprehending, awaiting the reactions of the others. But none came. Everyone carried on just as before, as though oblivious to this incredible outburst. As I was about to tiptoe shamefacedly away, the man looked up at me for the first time. What I interpreted as a wan smile flickered momentarily beneath the bushy eyebrows and wild grey eyes. He began to rummage in the depths of his jacket pocket and at length extracted a paper bag as wrinkled as his own face. I paused uncertainly; he appeared to be about to offer me a sweet. It would be downright bad manners to walk away now; I dithered, watching, yet pretending not to. The bag bulged open at last but it was not proffered in my direction. Instead, the man probed into it with impatient fingers and hurriedly transferred a quantity of its white contents to his mouth.

'Bloody heartburn,' he moaned, chomping hungrily.

I wandered in the direction of two younger men, who were poring over the pages of a shabby-looking notebook. To my relief, one of them looked up with a half-smile of acknowledgement.

'Take no notice of old Edwin,' he nodded towards the shrunken dyspeptic. 'This may be a madhouse but the other inmates are less violent.'

I gulped in gratitude. He explained that he was engaged in plotting the results of an underground survey carried out on the previous day, which would then be transposed on to one of the large linen plans to show the latest position of the workings. Mists of ignorance began to disperse before a shining beam of enlightenment; things began to fit into place.

'Mr. Wilkes will see you now,' a voice announced. I wheeled round to find a slender dark-haired girl framed in the doorway. And girls, too. An unexpected bonus, that; not the lacklustre, immature girls of my recent schooldays, but real sleek, sophisticated girls. I blinked in happy disbelief.

'If you'll come with me, please,' the mystery creature invited.

'I'll come with you anytime you like, Shirley,' someone called, as I hastened after the shapely retreating figure.

I was shown into an office bearing the name H. L. Wilkes on the door. The Area Chief Surveyor sat at a desk strewn with papers and documents, behind which were arranged shelves lined with heavy leather-bound books. A formidable-looking cabinet stood in one corner and the walls were covered with vast coloured plans of the kind I had seen earlier, interspersed with faded sepia-toned photographs depicting groups of complacent-looking men in bowler hats standing before towering pit headstocks.

11

Mr. Wilkes, poring with furrowed concentration over a sheet of paper, nodded absently towards a chair. I was struck at once by his finely-chiselled features and pale, almost delicate complexion. Mid-fiftyish, with steely-grey hair and moustache, his immaculate dress and appearance stood out in sharp contrast with his sombre, almost drab surroundings. I waited.

My lack of ability in maths, as revealed in my school report and exam results, was, it transpired, the cause of Mr. Wilkes's concern. Mathematics, he began to explain in a tone of voice and with a mastery of words totally beyond my experience, comprised the very foundation of the profession I aspired to enter. True, some aptitude at drawing and an interest in geology and economic geography would be useful, but maths was the key to the matter.

I sat with downcast eyes, humbled. The vision of a life of cricket, girls and manly fellowship, the exciting possibilities of which I had suddenly and blissfully become aware, seemed about to drift cruelly out of my reach. Father had been right, as always; I should have known. There remained merely the formality of dismissal.

Mr. Wilkes, however, had returned to the school report. 'They seem to think that your strength, if you have one, is in English,' he observed dryly, referring once more to my exam results. 'Umm - credit in language, yet only a pass in literature.' The frown returned. 'Ever done any acting?'

Acting? My thoughts were in turmoil. I'd once learned two of Stanley Holloway's monologues about a boy being eaten by a lion, with a view to reciting them at a school concert, only to excuse myself, through lack of confidence, on the day before the event. Better be honest.

'No sir - not really.' I confessed.

Mr. Wilkes didn't seem unduly concerned. 'You should try it. We have an excellent dramatic society at the Miners'

Welfare.' I mumbled appreciatively. 'Well, we'll take you on,' Mr. Wilkes said at length, traces of lingering doubt clearly discernible in his voice. 'You'll have to work hard at that maths, mind - better enrol for an evening class as well as your normal day-release at Nottingham Tech.'

I gulped my thanks and asked when I was to report for duty.

'Monday morning at nine o'clock,' came the reply. I turned to leave. The coveted vision, almost lost, had miraculously become a reality after all.

'Oh, by the way,' Mr. Wilkes called as I reached the door. 'I omitted to mention - you won't be based here. Report to Mr. Elliston, the Sub Area Surveyor at Swainsbrook Colliery.'

Shirley stood on the narrow landing, her back to the window. Beyond, the cricket field beckoned. I fought my way through a cloud of intoxicating perfume, stepping with exaggerated care around the twin distractions poised beneath the dark sweater. I floated down the stairs and out into the street. I had a job.

# Chapter 2

'**S**wainsbrook - what a stroke of luck!' Father beamed. 'Nice small office, and only just down the hill. Landed on your feet and no mistake.'

I saw what he meant. Nevertheless, being deprived of the peripheral benefits offered by a post at the area headquarters had in the meantime tempered my own enthusiasm to a considerable degree. Still, I had a job; that in itself was something.

Mother's misgivings had intensified now that my fate had been decided. No doubt they owed their origins to fears for my safety, stemming from a basic ignorance of the industry alongside which she had co-existed for over half a century. They emerged, however, as an obsessive preoccupation with cleanliness - or rather the lack of it - in my future career.

'There'll be his pit clothes to wash,' she pronounced in tones heavy with dread. 'I shan't know where to start.'

Father did his best to reassure her. 'He won't go down very often, Mother. And it'll only be around the pit bottom. Nothing but a bit of dust, that'll be all. You'll see.'

Mother's fears were not so easily allayed, however. 'And where will he wash and change?' she persisted.

Father reminded her that the Swainsbrook pithead baths had been opened before the outbreak of war.

'You mean........he'll have to strip and wash.....with all those....colliers?' she sniffed miserably.

Father struggled to keep his growing exasperation in check. 'It'll only be now and again, remember,' he coaxed. 'It'll be draughtsmanship most of the time, like I said before. You'll see.'

Our local colliery, I discovered on the following Monday morning, consisted not of one, but of four pits, scattered over a wide area, each hemmed in by its own group of soot-encrusted buildings.  One shaft only, New Pit, was used for coal extraction; the two others nearby, Deep Pit and Wright's Lane Pit, serving for ventilation and access purposes only.

The survey office, one of a cluster of low, single-storey, almost mellow buildings, was located nearly a mile distant. Nearby rose the squat headstocks over the fourth shaft, Old Pit, now used merely for pumping water.  Above towered a tapering chimney with its associated boilers, while a few other miscellaneous buildings completed the group.  The place was a backwater, an isolated outpost sinking into a state of dignified yet unmistakable decay.

I arrived to find the entire place deserted.  At my mother's prompting I had set off early to allow ample walking time. I had covered the distance comfortably in a quarter of an hour, yet was amazed to find myself on entirely unfamiliar ground. If, as appeared likely, this was to be my place of work for some considerable time, the sooner I became acquainted with it the better.  I began to look around.

Not all the buildings, I soon realised, belonged to the Coal Board. Until the nationalisation of the mines a few months before, the colliery had been part of the empire of the principal local landowner, whose country seat stood discreetly veiled in extensive parkland a couple of miles distant.  The administrative office, maintenance depot and sawmill of this estate, I now discovered, were situated adjacent to the group of buildings that included the survey office, but remained part of the squire's domain, as a notice indicated:

Swainsbrook Park Estate Office.

B. D. H. Playfair-Westwood, Proprietor.

T. F. Blore, Agent.

Just then the sawmill suddenly burst into activity, the whine of the circular saw shattering the stillness of the morning and drowning the whistles and chuckles of the starlings, whose vocalising had until then been the only sound. After wandering casually along the front of the buildings of which my future workplace formed a part, curiosity prompted me to crane my neck at the window of a substantial extension built on to the main structure and protruding at right angles from it. Thwarted in my intentions by the opaque glass comprising the lower half of the window, I climbed on to the sill and shielding my eyes, peered inside. What I saw caused me to boggle in disbelief. The walls of the entire room were decorated with large framed photographs of elegant women, a few in portrait form but the majority depicting small groups posing alluringly either in daringly provocative dresses or in 1930s-style bathing costumes.

I soon realised that the group photographs all had one feature in common. In the centre of each, clad in a pale suit and flamboyant wide-brimmed hat, his arms linked on each side with one of these gorgeous creatures, stood a portly, aristocratic-looking man. Dazed, I stepped back on to the ground. I had snatched a furtive glimpse of a way of life that in my innocence I had imagined existed only in such exotic places as Hollywood, and certainly not in the vicinity of a colliery village.

The survey office door stood ajar as I returned to the front of the block. The sight that met my eyes on entering resembled a scaled-down version of the drawing office at area headquarters - a long, low room with suspended lights, but with one immense table occupying virtually the entire floor-space. The lights had not yet been switched on and my eyes took some time to adjust to the gloomy interior, from which the opaque lower panes effectively excluded the early-morning sunshine.

Two faces loomed out of the half-light, each to my relief smiling in welcome. One belonged to a short, cherubic man of middle age and with a prodigious hooked nose, who introduced himself as Bert. The other, lean and fresh-complexioned, his dark wavy hair clearly receding, informed me he was Lionel. I learned too that, working under the sub-area surveyor, they were responsible for the surveying of Swainsbrook and two other nearby collieries. Apparently I was the first trainee to be appointed since nationalisation but another recruit would be commencing in a few weeks time.

'Three of us to cover three pits - it's hard work,' said Bert.

'And that's if you count the Old Man,' added Lionel. 'He doesn't go down much nowadays.'

'Of course, that's not including the linesmen,' Bert added.

'No, the linesmen are extra,' Lionel agreed.

Bewildered, I saw mental pictures of flag-waving, black-uniformed figures rushing around underground. 'Linesmen?' I queried.

'They're lads attached to the survey staff, but they work underground full time.' Bert explained.

'Good lads, some of them - do a lot of the donkey work,' Lionel reflected.

Bert nodded vigorously. 'Salt of the earth, a good linesman is.'

Suddenly an inner door opened and an elderly white-haired figure, dressed in a brown tweed jacket entered. Bert wheeled round attentively.

'Our new trainee's arrived, Mr. Elliston,' he said.

\*\*\*\*\*\*\*\*\*\*\*\*\*\*\*\*

I could not recall having my hand shaken before. And if I had, the memory faded beyond recall after experiencing one of Mr. Elliston's handshakes. For Mr. Elliston, as I was soon to find out, did nothing by halves. The steely grip, the methodical pumping and the sheer duration of the exercise made it memorable, to say nothing of the numbness of the fingers which persisted for some considerable time afterwards.

Mr. Elliston ushered me into his office, a poky yet almost cosy little room, deprived of light, like the others I had seen, by its opaque lower window. I was invited to sit, and for the first time that I could recall, encouraged to conduct a conversation with an adult member of my own sex. I was asked my views on a range of topics and chided good-humouredly when I expressed an opinion without being able to substantiate it with reasoned argument.

After a time, I became aware that I was actually talking, and with an increasing fluency, to this man. And Mr. Elliston was an attentive listener; the clear blue eyes set deep in the broad, slightly-bronzed face twinkled warmly from time to time and a gentle, almost furtive smile was quick to crease the wide, expressive lips.

Our informal introductory chat over, Mr. Elliston went on to outline the nature of my duties. To begin with, I would be working in the main office alongside Mr. Trouncer, whom I took to be Bert, and Lionel. Mr. Trouncer, Mr. Elliston explained, had served as his assistant at Swainsbrook for many years and would help me in every way he could. From time to time I would be called upon to carry out errands to the offices at the main colliery and sometimes further afield. Had I any questions? When would I make my first visit underground, I asked.

'In due course, my boy,' Mr. Elliston said, rising. He gave a slight nervous cough, a mannerism I had noticed earlier. 'We'll have another chat, you and I, before then.'

\*\*\*\*\*\*\*\*\*\*\*\*\*\*\*\*

The morning passed quickly. After watching Lionel plot, with what seemed effortless skill, the up-to-date position of a

18

coal face on a large plan similar to those I had seen at Area Headquarters, I was given a draughtsman's pen of my own and told to practice the art, first on paper, then on an unwanted scrap of linen. My first results were a depressing series of blots and smears, but gradually some semblance of jagged and irregular black lines began to emerge. Elated at this modest achievement, I pressed on.

Bert Trouncer reserved his judgment. 'Let's see how you get on with tracing,' he said.

I was given a plan of the layout of some underground workings and a sheet of tracing paper; this was more like the real thing - something to get my teeth into. I warmed to the task.

Meanwhile Bert sang. Lionel and I were treated to a lively, varied and continuous rendering of songs from the old-time music halls, obviously part of an extensive repertoire. And on the rare occasions when the words eluded his memory, Bert improvised with a range of vocal sounds representing the associated instruments - trumpet, trombone and euphonium. Lionel joined in with a few of the more popular choruses; not that Bert appeared to notice; he went about his work with, literally, a song on his lips, lapsing into silence only when some, to me, inaudible movement beyond the inner door indicated Mr. Elliston's approach.

Bert was already at the office when I arrived on the following morning, bustling around, whistling chirpily. His thick woollen socks were drawn up almost to knee height over his stumpy trousered legs; his battered black safety helmet, knee-pads and enormous steel toe-capped boots completed the picture.

A bulky wooden box with a leather strap and two heavy-looking wooden tripods with extendable legs stood by the outer door. There was a scrape of boots outside, followed by a breezy knock.

'My linesman,' explained Bert, then, raising his voice, 'Come in, Dan.'

A well-built, craggy-faced young man entered, dressed, like Bert, in pit clothes. A shock of auburn hair protruded from beneath his helmet, which he wore in a jaunty fashion on the back of his head. He grinned and proffered a ready hand as Bert introduced us. Conversation turned to pigs. Dan's father, I learned, had been compelled to leave the pit after being trapped in a roof fall, and now kept a few pigs on a smallholding, assisted by his son.

Bert shouldered the wooden box and Dan effortlessly picked up the tripods. I was engulfed in a strange mixture of admiration and envy as they set off for the pit.

The office seemed strangely quiet without Bert. Lionel, continuing to update a series of complex-looking plans, was affable enough. Perhaps I was missing the singing, for which Lionel's intermittent outbursts of currently popular numbers were an inadequate substitute.

I carried on with my tracing, and with relief discovered that my control over the pen was improving, to such a degree that I wanted to disown my efforts of the previous day. I now began to grasp a little of the significance of the plan I had been given to trace. It showed the extent of the workings of the nearby colliery in one particular seam. It was not until then that I noticed the position of the shaft. Stretching my meagre mathematical knowledge to the full, I calculated, by reference to the scale of the plan, that some of the workings extended well over a mile from the shaft bottom.

I consulted Lionel.

'A mile?' Lionel repeated in mild derision. 'A mile's nothing. Some faces are three miles or more out. Nothing more than a pleasant stroll, that.'

I recalled vaguely having seen a film showing miners

riding on a sort of miniature underground railway. 'You mean the men have to.....walk?' I ventured suspiciously.

Lionel nodded. 'That's right. The walking part's the easy bit - it's what comes after that makes you sweat.'

'And what does come after that?' I demanded.

Lionel smiled grimly. 'Hands and knees - and no bloody bumps-a-daisy,' came the reply.

After lunch, at Mr. Elliston's suggestion, Lionel gave me my first lesson in the use of the mining dial. He produced a wooden box similar to the one that Bert had taken underground, handed me a tripod, and led the way outside. After setting up the tripod, which he insisted I called the legs, he opened the box. The dial, I learned, was an instrument midway in sophistication between a compass and a theodolite. Equipped with two sighting vanes, it was used to carry out simple underground surveys and to indicate the new directions of the workings when a change of bearing was required. I was given practice in sighting various points around the vicinity and in reading the size of the angles through which the dial turned. The operation was somewhat more complicated in the darkness of the mine, Lionel informed me, where sighting involved the use of flame safety lamps suspended by screw hooks from the roof.

The gable of the room containing the gallery of photographs was visible from where we stood, and feigning innocence, I asked Lionel its purpose.

'That's the inner sanctum, that is,' came the cautious reply. 'Belongs to the Squire. Always kept locked. Him and Topsy Blore are the only ones with keys.' He indicated the notice outside the estate office.

I decided to reveal what I had seen on the previous morning. Lionel's face creased into a broad, disbelieving grin. He appeared to regard me with a newly-discovered interest.

'You crafty little bugger!' he exploded. 'Is that right?' Without waiting for a reply, he slipped quickly over to the window and after looking warily around, climbed on to the sill. He seemed to be perched there for an age, staring intently. I looked around uneasily. Dragging himself away at last, he returned, nodding his head in wonder.

'The randy old sod,' he mused slowly, in awe, his voice little more than a whisper.

'Enough crumpet there to satisfy an army - and to think I've been working here for six months and had missed that.' There was no trace of condemnation in his voice - only a blend of amazement and envy.

'Was that the Squire?' I asked. I seemed to recall hearing fanciful rumours of his many and varied exploits while still at school. It seemed that they were not so fanciful after all.

Lionel was still bemused. 'That's him.' He gave a solemn nod. 'Hefty great bloke - dresses in posh clothes - flabby purple face - no wonder!' He indicated the estate office. 'You'll see him. Rolls up in a bloody great hooded Pontiac to see Topsy Blore. Can't tell a word he says - half sozzled most of the time. Or shagged out.' He spoke the words with a kind of hushed reverence.

I was still far from clear how the Squire was able to obtain access to such an inexhaustible supply of beautiful women. I asked Lionel.

'It's money, isn't it?' he explained. 'They're not just any women, you know - famous actresses and society women, they are. And they go where the money is - simple as that.' He went on to relate an incident concerning the old squire which had been told to him by his father, who had once been a banksman at one of the Swainsbrook pits. Apparently a house party had been held at the nearby hall and two of the lady guests had expressed the wish to go down the pit. The old squire had not been very keen on the idea, knowing that he would need to accompany them, but had at last been persuaded to agree. Seeing the master with his charming guests approaching the shaft, the banksman ordered that coal-winding be immediately suspended and the cage made ready for its special duty.

Just as the old squire was about to lead his guests on to the cage, the banksman, noticing several small lumps of coal lying on the floor, grabbed a brush and began to sweep them out on to the loading platform. To the old squire - who had with great reluctance agreed to descend the pit, and to whom the interruption in coal-winding was a further source of irritation - this was the last straw. 'Get out of the way, man!' he bawled. 'We can't be bothered with that. Time means money in my world and if my friends don't know that, then it's high time that they did.'

I alluded to the fact that the old era was now over. Lionel nodded wistfully.

'Of course he's raked off enough compensation money to last his time out. He'll be selling up here and be off to the Riviera if he's any sense.' he said.

Reflectively, reluctantly, we went back to our surveying.

# Chapter 3

We had lunch in the staff canteen. It was a cheerful and at times boisterous meal with one particular group, who I learned later were the time clerks, responsible for most of the bonhomie. We were served by a bevy of matronly aproned women, who responded to any jocularity aimed in their direction with a mixture of blushes, giggles and suppressed mirth, which was finally released in a series of near-hysterical squeals of laughter once they were back in the secure anonymity of the kitchen.

Mr. Elliston, I soon noticed, took no part in these proceedings. He had officially introduced me to the manageress on my first day, and often chatted easily enough with individual women, but his unease at the prolonged high-spiritedness was clearly apparent; his colour rose, he fidgeted in his seat, and the nervous cough was increasingly in evidence. On one such occasion, when suet dumplings were being served, the double-entendre remark made to the amply-built lady bending over one of the tables gave rise to more hilarity than usual. Inadvertently catching my superior's eye, I felt my own embarrassment rising at his obvious discomfiture. Lionel kicked my foot under the table.

'The Old Man's worried in case you get corrupted,' he said under his breath. '- not that he need bother.'

Misjudged as I was, I felt a certain amount of elation at being credited with such worldliness by someone several years my senior. I was well aware that I owed this reputation to the chance discovery of the contents of the inner sanctum; how long it would survive without some further evidence of my maturity I couldn't tell. My problem was compounded by my desire, not only to conform to Lionel's standards, but also to please Mr. Elliston, who had placed such trust in me. How long could I keep up this balancing act before coming the inevitable cropper?

****************

It was Mr. Elliston's suggestion that I should start cycling to work. He pointed out that not only would I save time getting to and from the office but that I should need a cycle to cover the ground quickly when I had to carry out errands during the day. Bert and Lionel left their bikes outside, leaning against the office wall; Mr. Elliston, however, kept his in a small outbuilding behind the block. It was an ancient model, painted completely white, a relic of the war years, when its owner had been an air-raid warden.

One morning, after I had dismounted and was about to remove my cycle clips at the door, Bert's gnome-like face appeared. 'Don't bother taking them off,' he called, 'We're doing the grand tour.'

I had been told that one day soon I would be taken to visit the different offices and workshops scattered around the colliery. I had assumed for some reason that Mr. Elliston would be conducting me and recalling the embarrassing incident in the canteen, was secretly relieved that my guide was to be Bert instead. I wondered if he would sing as we rode.

Bert grabbed his cycle by the handlebars but made no attempt to mount. 'The first port of call's the land-sale,' he said '- just round the corner. Come on.'

We stopped before a green door at the end of the block, which seemed permanently closed. An immaculate squat black Austin saloon of pre-war vintage stood outside. Bert tapped lightly and turned the handle. 'Mr. Degg - he keeps tabs on how much coal is sold and who buys it,' he explained as I followed him inside.

But it was not on Mr. Degg that my eyes fell as I entered

25

the dingy little office. Seated behind a typewriter facing us was a girl - a pretty, blushing, smiling girl. I hovered, lips dry, consumed with smouldering self-consciousness. Bert, however, was shackled by no such inhibitions. 'Morning, Enid love!' he sang out gaily. 'This is the bright new chap who's come to show us how it's done.'

I could have killed the chirpy, cheerful, harmless little man, standing there, eyes twinkling, oblivious to my misery. Looking somewhere between the girl's feet and the inner door, from beyond which a man's voice rumbled, I proffered a limp hand and an inaudible mutter of greeting. Enid reciprocated. Still the distant monologue droned.

'We'll wait until he's finished,' said Bert nonchalantly. Enid sat back at her typewriter, hesitating. 'Still come to work on that spanking new bike of yours?' Bert asked chattily. Enid whispered an affirmative. Bert nodded. 'And still biking home for lunch, eh? Should manage to keep fit, that way.' He threw me a quick provocative glance. My heart sank, waiting for the worst. 'Gordon here's a keen cyclist – special bike. You two'll have to fix something up one of these days.'

It was Enid who ended the agony. 'Mr. Degg is free now - I think.' Responding to the situation, her speech was suddenly clear, urgent. She leapt up, tapped, and opened the door.

Mr. Degg - florid, elderly, with forlorn sagging jowls and a voice combining depth of pitch with monotony of tone - shook my hand absently, said that my surname sounded familiar and wished us a rumbling good morning. Bert lingered for another word with Enid on the way out. I waited, fuming, by the battered old Hercules sit-up-and-beg I had inherited from Father.

'Nice girl is Enid,' said Bert, mounting his cycle. 'Thought I'd put you a good word in.' He winked mischievously.

We spent the rest of the morning picking our way, sometimes on our cycles, more often on foot, along what seemed to me a bewildering labyrinth of narrow, twisting dirt-trodden paths by which the various colliery buildings were connected. This layout appeared to lack any semblance of order; the pitted and soot-encrusted buildings with their grey slate roofs were strewn around haphazardly, with the intervening spaces cluttered with discarded and rusting equipment and machinery. Our ears were assailed by the continuous hiss of escaping steam, punctuated by an intermittent cacophony of screechings, clankings and bangings, the more violent of which caused the ground itself to tremble alarmingly.

Puddles of foul-smelling water, half-hidden by a film of coal dust, lay in every slight depression, as though awaiting the carelessly-placed foot. There was also a steady drip of water, some of it disconcertingly hot, from a tangle of overhead pipes and gutterings. Even more unpleasant was the evil smear of greasy oil with which everything seemed to be coated. This varied to the touch from an insidious pitch-like substance - which when mixed with coal dust produced a combination guaranteed to stain anything with which it made contact - to a vile-odoured yellowish lubricant, which lay around in a collection of battered buckets, constant pitfalls for the unwary.

It seemed at first that this vast, sprawling, noisy, stinking monster was some kind of robot, fulfilling some obscure function by its own momentum, independent of human action. Gradually, however, I became aware of a legion of men, drab and grimy, living out their working lives in the twilight world beneath the pipes and gantries. I began to see doors open, wheels turn, to notice anonymous figures wielding shovels, hammers and oil-cans - human cogs in this filthy, grinding, satanic place. And all this was literally on the surface; how would I find the underground world that awaited me?

Bert pressed on undeterred. I soon lost count of the grubby little buildings we visited and of the men, and their occupations, we met. The calls, however, followed a similar pattern. After introducing me briefly, Bert went on to what, for him, was clearly the most important part of the exercise, the swapping of humorous stories. I soon discovered that Bert's repertoire of these was just as extensive as his collection of music-hall songs. But whereas the songs kept roughly within certain acceptable limits of taste, the stories and jokes were bound by no similar conventions. This is not to say that all Bert's tales were dirty; a good number were, but their coarseness was softened - made to sound almost innocent even - by the series of nods, winks, grins, chuckles, and digs in the ribs which accompanied them.

Bert, I noticed, never actually swore. As a true and natural comic, he relied on timing, allusion and gesture. Nor did he implicate individual personalities in his humour; he heard out with a fixed grin of politeness the many wisecracks concerning specific womenfolk, but was quick to re-direct the course of the exchanges when the opportunity presented itself.

On one occasion, his lack of sympathy with the tone of conversation was such that his customary politeness and patience were stretched to their limits. We were in the fitting shop, a vast barn-like building in which coal cutters, conveyor engine motors and other items of underground equipment were repaired. The usual introductions had been made and a florid-faced man with bushy-grey eyebrows and a rasping voice began monopolising the exchanges, using a range of obscenities to describe his sexual prowess, obviously putting on some sort of show for my benefit. Evading Bert's attempts to intervene, the man then turned his attention to Enid, embarking on an explicit account of what he would like to do to her. This was more than Bert could stand. The smile, and colour too, faded from his face; he took his leave tersely and to my relief, I found myself standing outside, eyeing, thankfully almost, the sooty walls, greasy girders and hideous, hopeless surroundings.

'Take no notice of Matt Mason,' Bert advised. 'It's all talk - his missus is gaffer at their house. Old Matt daren't say so much as 'Boo' when she's around.' He half-turned and I heard the jet hit the ground. 'Let's go and see Claude Millin,' he said, buttoning up. 'There'll be no dirty talk there, I'll tell you.'

The saddler's shop was small, dark and quiet. Situated on the edge of the colliery, and reached by a cinder path which led eventually to a small paddock in which the pit ponies were let out to graze during the annual holiday, it was quite unlike any of the other buildings I had visited. Mr. Millin was something of an individual too. A bent, wrinkled little man with a tuft of white hair like a plume of smoke on the top of his head, he groped forward to meet us through a festooning barrier of leather.

There were bridles, straps of every description, thongs, belts - all hanging from the undulating whitewashed ceiling, stacked on the surrounding shelves, piled on the bench, even heaped on the irregular stone-flagged floor. Claude Millin squinted up enquiringly through tiny oval glasses and after listening to Bert's words of introduction, proffered a skinny hand of greeting.

'Working with Mister Elliston, eh?' he beamed. 'A real gentleman, he is, and no mistake. You'll be alright with Mister Elliston.' I noticed several biblical texts pinned around the walls of the little workshop and remarked on this to Bert as we re-mounted our cycles.

'Lay preacher is Claude - Primitive Methodist,' Bert said.

'Takes services at little chapels miles away - up in the Peak, some of them. Walks every yard of the way, too.'

He went on to tell me that the old saddler had made his pit belt and kneepads, as he had Mr. Elliston's, but that this practice had been discontinued since nationalisation. 'We have to make do with mass-produced stuff from the stores now,' Bert added regretfully. 'Which reminds me, we'd better call there and get you fixed up while we're about it.'

The stores, a vast, newly-erected building near the main shaft, stocked an enormous range of equipment. I was issued with a black lightweight safety helmet, which I was told was made from compressed cardboard; a pair of safety boots with steel toecaps; and a pair of rubber kneepads. The weight of the boots appalled me; they felt as though they were anchoring my feet to the ground. How I would ever be able to walk in them I had no idea. So much for Father's vague notion of occasional brief joyrides to the pit bottom. The fact that I was being issued with all this equipment seemed to indicate that my mining experience was to be rather more extensive than he had predicted.

Trying out my kneepads prompted my thoughts to turn to cricket. The buckled straps were not unlike those of cricket pads......I would join the colliery welfare cricket club in the following spring. It was a well-known fact that pitmen made good cricketers, especially fast bowlers. And above all else, I wanted to be a fast bowler; I had built up a fair amount of pace on the bald and bumpy corner of waste ground on which we had played at dinner times during my last year at school. Next season I would set my sights on the big time, and when the county's call came, I'd be ready.

Bert cut my daydreams short. 'Pithead baths next stop,' he said briskly. 'Get you fixed up with a locker. Come on.' We made our way towards a large, modern building behind the canteen. 'We'll go in the dirty side,' Bert said, 'and come out the clean end.'

I soon found out what he meant. The changing areas were divided into two parts, one for working clothes, the other for ordinary dress. The showers were situated between the two areas. Each man therefore had two lockers, opened by the same key. At Bert's suggestion, I put my pads and helmet in my work locker and my boots on the rack beneath.

'Better look out some pit clothes,' Bert advised. 'Mr. Elliston may be going down next week and I've an idea that he'll be taking you with him.' I studied the heels of my new boots protruding from the rack.

'Oh - good,' I replied, in a voice intended to suggest if not enthusiasm, then at least a degree of confidence.

Bert was in his element in the time office. The clerks were a cheerful bunch and the repartee flowed thick and fast. I had noticed that Mr. Elliston's presence tended to cramp Bert's style in the canteen when the clerks were up to their usual antics. Now, however, his stature as a natural clown was fully revealed. Aided and abetted by two of the younger clerks, he proceeded to stage a display of spontaneous slapstick comedy that had the rest of us in uncontrollable laughter. We were treated to animal impressions, songs, jokes, impersonations and, as we were about to leave, a series of cartwheels which, considering that the performer appeared to be well into his fifties, were quite an achievement.

'A quick peep into the lamp cabin and we'll call it a day,' Bert said as we emerged from the time office. Still weak from mirth, I followed.

Nowhere was my ignorance of the world of mining more exposed than in the lamp-room. I knew from my conversation with Lionel that flame safety lamps of the kind invented by Sir Humphrey Davy were still used both to indicate dangerous gas and in surveying. What I had not realised was how heavy and inefficient were the electric hand-lamps issued to the miners.  I had expected to see the modern lightweight battery-and-cable cap lamps, as depicted in N.C.B. propaganda; these, I was told, would not be arriving at Swainsbrook until a new automatically-recharging lamp-room had been built.  How would I manage to move around below ground in my steel-capped boots, carrying a set of heavy, bulky surveying legs and an antique lamp - made, if its weight was anything to go by - of cast iron?  I felt faint at the thought.

The lamp-room attendant beckoned me over to a huge board covering the entire wall.  It bristled with small numbered hooks, some of which held two similarly-numbered metal discs.

'Tha' number's 1186,' he said.  I turned blankly to Bert.

'It's your check number,' he explained.  'You collect your discs with your lamp and give one to the banksman when you go down.'  The attendant, a lean, sombre-looking man in overalls, clearly believed in leaving no scope for misinterpretation.

'If there's only one check on that 'ook, we know tha's down there', he pronounced grimly.  'Tha' musna' lose it - if owt 'appens, th' search party'll need it to identify thee.'

My throat went dry.  What before had been comfortingly vague and remote suddenly took on a stark, alarming reality.

# Chapter 4

The promised chat with Mr. Elliston, in which I had assumed he intended to brief me on matters relating to personal safety and the nature of my duties underground, took place a few days later. I was ushered once more into the tiny office, offered a chair opposite my superior's desk, and subjected to a lengthy and rigorous interview - on my knowledge of cricket.

Apparently something I had said a day or two earlier to Bert Trouncer, extolling a game which clearly meant little or nothing to him, had been reported faithfully to - and received enthusiastically by - my superior. He had, he told me, been a keen player himself in his younger days and was now an enthusiastic spectator of and above all, reader about the game. Had I, he wondered, encountered the writings of Neville Cardus in *The Manchester Guardian*? No? Then he would bring me some pieces to peruse. Was I familiar with Wisden? My blank response prompted the offer of a loan of one, whatever it might be.

To my relief, Mr Elliston switched to my own cricketing aspirations. I felt on safer ground here and volunteered the fact that my ambition was to make my mark as a left-arm pace bowler in the tradition of Clark, of Northants and Voce, of Notts. Mr Elliston gave a slow reflective nod. He, too, he confessed, had once entertained hopes of achieving success as a fast bowler before applying himself to the more subtle craft of spin.

'As a left hander, you would do well to consider learning the spin bowler's art,' Mr Elliston advised. 'What a pity that you missed seeing the late Hedley Verity in action. His death in the war was a tragic loss.' Instantly I recalled the great Yorkshireman's picture in my cigarette card collection. 'Anyway, you may care to give the matter some thought,' my superior went on. 'I wish you success whatever you decide and I'm delighted that you are an enthusiast for our great summer game.'

'But there is another matter that we must discuss', Mr. Elliston indicated with a cough, the colour rising to his face. 'You......er.....will be going down the pit shortly, and.....er..... will encounter certain.....er..... behaviour on the part of others below ground that, er.....might.....er.....shock.....er.....and even tempt you to.....er.....indulge .....er..... in the kind of language unworthy of, er.....' Mr. Elliston's own uneasiness began to affect me too. We sat facing one another in the dark, poky little room, my superior blushing and stammering miserably, unable to terminate an ordeal that he had embarked upon with the very best of intentions but that was now in danger of degenerating into pure farce.

After what seemed an age, I stumbled on uneasy legs, cheeks tingling, back into the drawing office, my jumbled thoughts divided between achieving distinction on the cricket field and avoiding the bottomless pit of iniquity that beckoned not far away. As to what lay ahead on my first visit underground, I remained as ignorant as before.

But not for long. The following day, Mr. Elliston announced that he would be descending the New Pit on Saturday morning to assess the progress of a stone-heading not far from the pit bottom, and that I would be accompanying him . Bert Trouncer's moon face beamed at me across the table as the inner door closed.

'There you are - a nice gentle start. Couldn't be better!'

What I had intended as a confident smile obviously failed to register as such.

'You'll only be down for a couple of hours at the most - not long enough to get your face black.'

'Does that mean I'll not need to put on my pit clothes?' I ventured.

Lionel erupted into an outburst of incredulous laughter, while Bert dropped his rueful smile and attempted to explain. 'You *always* put on your pit clothes when you go down, even if you intend coming back up again straight away,' he began with an exaggerated show of patience. 'Pits are dirty places - and dangerous too.' Lionel's fast-balding head was still swaying from side to side in silent disbelief. A sudden, intriguing thought struck me. With my devastating ignorance already fully exposed, I had nothing to lose.

'And will Mr. Elliston be getting changed too?'

The two exchanged mirthful, knowing glances. 'He will, that,' Bert chuckled, '- but you won't see him doing it.'

'Unless you peep through his keyhole,' Lionel added, indicating the inner door.

And so, early on the following Saturday morning, instead of reporting at the survey office as usual, I left my bike in the cycle shed by the canteen and made my way into the pithead baths. Coal production had ended for the week and the only work taking place underground was concerned with maintenance. As the men engaged on this were already at work, I had the changing rooms to myself and was able to don my pit clothes unobserved. At last, booted, knee-padded and helmeted, I emerged once more into the pit yard and set off self-consciously for the lamp room, where I was to meet Mr. Elliston, who, as Bert and Lionel had intimated, would have changed into his pit clothes in his office.

It took merely a few steps for me to discover just how heavy and cumbersome were my steel toe-capped boots. Every stride required a conscious effort and the normally simple matter of lifting the feet to avoid tripping over an obstacle such as a railway track suddenly became a test of strength and physical co-ordination. How on earth would I cope underground? Hopefully, as well as countless others who had faced a similar situation before me; at least, my initiation into pit life was, by all accounts, to be a gentle one.

I could see Mr. Elliston's white bicycle leaning against the lamp- room wall and instinctively quickened my pace - or rather, tried to.    To my dismay, I realised that such acceleration was beyond my physical capabilities. Instead, I plodded on anxiously. I needn't have worried.  As I entered the building I could see my superior, clad in helmet, well-cut jacket and with long woollen stockings drawn up towards his knees, engaged in conversation with the cadaverous-looking man I had encountered on my tour with Bert.    Hovering closer, it became apparent that cricket was the topic under discussion, with the county side's fortunes being subjected to a detailed critical analysis.  Clearly Mr. Elliston's opinions were being heard with respect; his every pronouncement being greeted by 'I quite agree, Mr. Elliston', 'that's right, Mr. Elliston,' and similar variations, all uttered in tones far removed from the forthright manner in which I had been received a few days earlier.

Soon, equipped with our lamps, we set off towards the shaft headstocks, towering with a stark geometrical impressiveness high above the other buildings. Mr. Elliston, I noticed, carried a small lightweight lamp, whereas mine was one of the ancient, bulky hand lamps I had seen earlier. Drawing nearer the shaft, I realised for the first time that instead of the cage loading platform being at ground level, we would be climbing a series of metal steps leading to a covered area half as high as the headgear itself - going up, in other words, before going down.  It seemed a trifle pointless but I decided not to raise the matter with Mr. Elliston, for fear of adding to the gaffes I had made already in my dialogue with Bert and Lionel.  Not that I would have stood much chance of interjecting my question.  For Mr. Elliston kept up a continuous commentary on the features we passed on our way, interspersed with thumbnail sketches of the occupations of the various men we encountered, all of whom greeted him with a respectful 'Mornin', Mester Elliston,' and were answered without exception by their Christian names.

Although no coal winding was taking place, the wheels seemed to be spinning continuously and the resulting vibration caused the steps to shake alarmingly as we climbed. Grimly clutching the hand-rail, I endeavoured to drag my steel-encased feet alongside those of my elderly superior, who to my surprise was wearing ordinary boots, unencumbered by heavy toe-caps and whose legs were free of the pads whose straps were already chafing the backs of my own knees.

At last, having reached the loading deck, we advanced towards the waiting cage. Before stepping on board however, we handed over one of our check- number discs and submitted to the routine contraband search by the banksman, who, I noticed, subjected Mr. Elliston's pockets to the lightest of taps after having felt comprehensively into and around my own.

Although the metal cage was large enough to hold upwards of a dozen men, we were the only two descending. I stood with my free hand gripping the handrail and my feet apart, endeavouring to keep my trembling legs bent slightly at the knee, as I had been advised. I tried to shut out of my mind the fact that the metal plate beneath my feet was all that separated me from the shaft bottom, 420 yards below. 420 yards. I was willing myself to calculate the number of cricket pitches that represented when in response to the banksman's signal, the cage rose slightly from its safety catches before plummeting down into the echoing darkness.

Aware of my tenseness, Mr. Elliston prepared me in calming tones for two sensations that were shortly to assail me as we plunged. It was fortunate that he did, otherwise the eerie swish of the other, rising cage, passed half-way down the shaft, followed soon afterwards by the violent sideways lurch as we negotiated a kink in the shaft at an old working level, would have reduced me to something approaching a nervous wreck. As it was, the ride, though alarming in the speed of its descent, confined its effects to my ears. They popped for some time afterwards, lending the voices of those I met underground a strange faraway quality that somehow seemed in keeping with this subterranean world.

After yet another frisking of our pockets, I followed Mr. Elliston along the high semicircular main roadway leading from the shaft bottom towards the workings. Bright electric lights overhead made our lamps seem superfluous. Apart from the tramway rails, the rock floor was clear of obstructions, level, and although dusty, easy to walk on. The air, to my surprise, was pleasantly fresh. Even allowing for my popping ears, the silence was so complete as to seem almost oppressive. The change, when it finally came, amounted to a transformation. No sooner had we passed the last of the overhead lights at a junction and plunged into inky blackness, than the tunnel - or roadway as I soon learned to call it - was reduced to little over six feet in height and proceeded to dip steeply.

It was now that the shortcomings of my antiquated lamp were fully exposed. While my superior plodded steadily on, I found myself having to lift my lead-weight feet over the irregularly-laid wooden sleepers with the aid of a light which now seemed little better than a candle. To make matters worse, Mr. Elliston paused from time to time in his otherwise continuous discourse, as though allowing time for my brief response, and as the gap between us widened, and the monologue grew fainter, I found it increasingly difficult to insert my replies in the correct place.

At last, the flickering of distant lights appeared ahead and to my relief the gradient began to level out. Soon we arrived at the new heading, where five or six men were setting roof supports and packing huge slabs of rock along the sides of the recently begun roadway. To my surprise, a set of surveying legs were already in place and the light of my lamp revealed the craggy features of Dan, the linesman who had accompanied Bert underground on the morning of my second day at the office. He had, I learned, brought the two sets of legs and the heavy dial box down an hour or so earlier, and had already set up the equipment in readiness for our arrival. I gathered that this was partly to spare me the task of struggling with these bulky items on my first trip underground. Next time, it was made clear, I would be expected to do my share of the carrying.

After exchanging the time of day with each workman and inquiring after the health of Dan's father, Mr. Elliston got down to business. This, as Lionel had explained to me earlier, entailed measuring angles by sighting distant oil lamps suspended from the roof of the main roadway and to achieve this, the men were requested to switch off their lamps. I now realised for the first time in my life the true meaning of the term inky blackness. For apart from Mr. Elliston's own lamp, which he switched on from time to time to record the bearings in his notebook, we stood in utter darkness, rendered even more dramatic by the self-imposed silence of the men, who stood, patient and respectful, until our work was completed.

Once the bearing of the new heading had been established, Dan produced a hand-drill, plugs, a length of string and a can of whitewash and brush. I was sent to retrieve the oil lamps, one of which was used to project the shadow of the string - by then suspended from two plugs - on to the roof. I now discovered why Dan's job of linesman was so called; taking his brush, he proceeded to paint a neat white line on the roof, indicating to the men the exact bearing that the new heading was to be driven. He would then advance the line at regular intervals, thus ensuring that the heading progressed on its correct course.

Our work completed, we set off on the return journey to the pit bottom. This time, I had been given a set of legs to carry and their weight, together with that of my lamp, reduced me to a lurching stagger as we climbed the gradient back to the main roadway. The relief I experienced as the lights of this stretch of the route came into view was matched only by that felt as we finally arrived in the pit bottom. Aching, weary, I stepped off the cage into the sunshine of a late summer morning. We'd been underground for a little over two hours. After depositing our lamps and equipment, and taking leave of Mr. Elliston, who cycled off to his private changing room at the offices, Dan and I made our way towards the pithead baths.

'You've hardly got mucky,' Dan observed as we entered the changing rooms. 'Wait till you go down on a coal-turning shift.' It was not until I ruefully inspected my feet after thankfully kicking off the loathsome boots that it suddenly dawned on me - I'd been down a coal mine but I hadn't seen a single lump of coal.

# Chapter 5

Day-to-day life in the survey office continued uneventfully throughout the summer months. Bert sang, Lionel occasionally accompanied him, Mr. Elliston appeared from time to time through the connecting doors, while I burrowed ever deeper into the mysteries of Box Five.

Box Five was a huge, compartmentalised plan chest that stood in one corner of the room. It contained assorted bundles of rolled linen plans, many of considerable antiquity, dealing with every aspect of the Swainsbrook Park Estate. My task was to open each bundle, summarise its contents, label each individual plan, and extract everything not directly concerned with the colliery for eventual transfer to the nearby estate office.

While most of the dusty and obscure plans, relating as they did to sales of land and similar transactions, contained little of interest, a few provided intriguing insights into a world of which until now I was blissfully unaware. One finely-drawn accident plan pulled me up in fascinated horror. It had been drawn as the official record of a grisly accident that had taken place at the Old Pit close by in the early years of the century, and depicted the battered remains of a pit cage that had somehow become unhooked from the winding rope and had plunged down the shaft, killing the four men it carried. Not content with his detailed impression of the smashed cage, the long-departed draughtsman had included the mangled corpses of the unfortunate occupants, using full colour to give maximum effect to his handiwork.

Later, I came upon a large-scale plan of proposed alterations to Swainsbrook Hall, which had been carried out during the lifetime of the father of the present squire. This proved to be of considerable interest to Lionel, who having marvelled at the distance separating the squire's bedroom from the boudoir of his lady, was giving Bert and me an entertaining impression of the old squire's nocturnal attempt to locate his beloved's chamber after an evening's dedicated drinking, when the door opened to reveal the disapproving frown of a florid and coughing Mr. Elliston.

Occasionally, during the following weeks, my discoveries in the depths of Box Five prompted a visit from Topsy Blore. The squire's agent, a pompous, bald-headed little man clad in gaudy check plus-fours, a scented handkerchief flopping from his top pocket, would descend on the office without warning and demand to examine the latest batch of unearthed plans relating to the estate. Mr. Elliston, I noticed, was co-operative though cool, bearing out Bert's assertion that he preferred dealing with the organ-grinder rather than with the monkey.

Topsy's departure was the signal for Lionel to give the office door several vigorous to-and-fro swings in an attempt to disperse the cloud of scent which permeated the room, while Bert screwed up his huge nose in distaste. I was surprised to see that this little ritual occasionally took place in Mr. Elliston's presence and although he played no part in it, I detected an approving half-smile and twinkle of the eye as he returned to his office.

And then, one afternoon, the organ-grinder himself graced us with his presence. The screech of brakes outside, followed by the slam of a car door, heralded the arrival of the Squire. There was a heavy footfall in the doorway and a huge figure lumbered into the room, demanding to see 'Elson.' The cut of his clothes, the whiff of scent, and general appearance reminded me of a larger-than-life version of Topsy Blore. The Squire, however, wore a wide-brimmed hat similar to that on his photographs lining the walls of the inner sanctum. And whereas his agent's voice was a high-pitched affected sneer, that of the Squire was a sonorous bark, slurred and almost incoherent, presumably by the effects of alcohol. Even so, I found the resemblance between the two men striking and remarked on it later to Lionel.

'Well, you know what they say,' came the reply. 'The old squire liked to spread it around and Topsy was his little gift to one of his fancy pieces.' I pondered on the implication of this. Clearly Lionel considered I needed further enlightenment. 'Topsy's only half size and half a brother,' adding as an afterthought, '- but he's not half a bastard!'

\*\*\*\*\*\*\*\*\*\*\*\*\*\*\*\*

As well as Swainsbrook, Mr. Elliston and his staff were responsible for surveying two other nearby collieries, and it was down one of these, Birch Park, that soon afterwards I experienced my first full shift underground. A much smaller mine than Swainsbrook, Birch Park had been sunk in Victorian times and was approaching the end of its productive life. Its owners prior to nationalisation had invested very little in it, with the result that it was badly in need of modernisation, a state of affairs that even I could appreciate.

As a first step towards breathing new life into Birch Park, the Coal Board had decided to open up a new three-foot seam, called appropriately the yard, and Mr. Elliston assigned Lionel, now well advanced in his studies to become a qualified surveyor, to carry out a detailed survey of the new development. A staff car from Swainsbrook was laid on to take Lionel and myself, together with our equipment, the short distance to Birch Park, where we were met by Colin, the linesman based at the colliery.

The sight of coal, which had somehow eluded me on my brief underground initiation at Swainsbrook, was everywhere apparent as we approached the pit-head. Trains of small trucks, which I soon learned to call tubs, were carrying loads of the stuff from the rapidly surfacing cages and depositing it at a tipping point into a vast screening plant. Dust and spilt slack lay everywhere and the faces of the men bustling purposefully around the shaft top were so blackened as to appear unrecognisable.

It was almost a relief to exchange the dust and din of the pithead for the cage, which plummeted us into the echoing darkness at a speed which, I was assured, was much slower than that at which coal-winding was carried out. Lionel had showed me a plan of the new workings and I thought I had prepared myself for what appeared to be about a mile of walking. What I had not allowed for was the speed at which I would be expected to travel and the difficulty of carrying so much tackle. Keeping pace with Mr. Elliston had been hard enough; now I found myself trailing behind two young men well used to striding along underground roadways, despite being loaded down with heavy, cumbersome surveying equipment. My own share of the load was modest - a set of legs, my hand lamp, flame lamp and my haversack - yet I found this burden a tremendous handicap when endeavouring to cover the uneven ground by the light of a primitive, hand-held lamp.

Once we had left the main roadway from the pit bottom, I encountered another obstacle. The roadway we now followed was a haulage road, along which trains of tubs travelled, clipped to a moving steel rope. This rope had the disconcerting habit of rising up without warning and falling back to hit the floor with a crack like a whiplash and this necessitated treading warily along the side of the roadway to avoid being sliced in half. Refuge holes had been left in the roadway sides at intervals and we took shelter in these at the ominous sound of approaching trains, rattling towards us through the darkness.

The new development, when we finally reached it, was a scene of bustling activity. An electric drill whined, tubs were being loaded with massive lumps of grey rock, men were erecting huge semicircular supports and a pony stood motionless in the darkness awaiting the unloading of its tub-full of timber. But what struck me most was the dust; not coal dust but clouds of fine all-pervading rock dust from the drilling, that irritated the throat and settled in a powdery layer on faces, clothing - everything.

And instead of the respectful cessation of activity that I had witnessed at Swainsbrook with Mr. Elliston, we had to carry out our work in the midst of all this noise and confusion. This meant calling to one another in loud shouts, which even then were scarcely audible above the din. My role, as the least experienced of the trio, was that of back-sight man. This involved bringing forward the rear set of legs and flame-lamp on receiving Lionel's distant signal. Meanwhile Colin had gone on ahead with the fore-sight legs. To ensure the accuracy of the sighting I had to wait with my lamp switched off, while at the same time watching for Lionel's signal - a side-to-side sweep of his own lamp. In normal circumstances, no doubt this method worked well enough but with so many other lights moving at random, I found it difficult to identify his from the rest. Fearful of uprooting the legs prematurely, I waited, my eyes straining into the darkness, unaware of Lionel's impatience with my excessive caution. Waiting until we were within earshot of a group of men, he launched into a tirade of abuse, accusing me among other things, of dozing at my work and of hindering progress generally. Sometime later I learned that the public humiliation of a new hand was considered perfectly normal in all departments of the industry. I had, in fact, got off extremely lightly; the usual initiation for a pit boy was to have his trousers pulled down and his genitals smeared with axle grease, to the gleeful cheers of his workmates.

Still stinging from the verbal blows I had received from him a short time before, I was surprised when Lionel waited for me after the next sighting to ask quite affably if I was getting hungry. It was not until I had perched thankfully alongside my workmates on a stack of pit props and opened my snap tin that I became fully aware of the keenness of my appetite. Noticing both Lionel and Colin use the first swig from their water bottles as a mouthwash, I followed suit and then tucked in - filthy hands and dust-laden air notwithstanding - to the carefully wrapped sandwiches Mother had packed.

The final stage of our day's work was to paint a white roof line similar to that I had seen at Swainsbrook. First, however, we had to await the detonation of an explosive charge, which rendered visibility virtually impossible. Resigned to the delay, Lionel and Colin squatted down with a group of other men. Friendly banter ensued and chewing tobacco - 'baccy' - was produced and handed round. Lionel and Colin, obviously familiar with it, accepted a piece readily and I was persuaded to give it a try. It took one tentative nibble to convince me that its taste was as loathsome as its appearance and my splutter of disgust gave rise to good-natured jeers of delight as lamps were turned in my direction.

'Dirty 'abit, is chewin'', one man volunteered, reaching into his pocket. 'Ere, lad - try a pinch o' snuff. This'll clear yer passages in no time.'

Following his example, I transferred a few grains of the powdery substance from my fingertips to the back of my wrist and inhaled deeply. The resulting violent sneezes added to the laughter which had not yet subsided following my initiation into tobacco-chewing.

46

Our day's labour finished at last, we set off for the pit bottom by a different route, eventually reaching a roadway along which a conveyor was carrying coal from one of the faces. Here, after watching a demonstration by Colin of how to jump on and from the moving belt, I followed my companions through the darkness. I was kept awake by the rhythmic pressure of the belt over the rollers as I lay face downwards on a bed of fine slack and coal dust, mentally rehearsing how I would leap clear and retrieve my equipment before the belt climbed roof-wards to pour its contents into the waiting tubs at the approaching junction.

\*\*\*\*\*\*\*\*\*\*\*\*\*\*\*\*\*

Wearily I pushed my bike into the shed, trudged across the yard and opened the kitchen door.

'Did you enjoy your snap?' Mother asked, and then, without waiting for an answer, scrutinised my face. 'You've got rings of dust round your eyes,' she announced accusingly. 'I thought you're supposed to have had a wash - a cat-lick, more likely. I wonder what state your towel's in. How I'm going to get your things clean if this is what it's going to be like, I just don't know.'

I left her chuntering, kicked off my shoes and padded towards the living-room sofa. I seemed to have been fending off sleep for an age. I could hold out no longer.

# Chapter 6

My inauspicious start as a trainee colliery surveyor was as nothing compared with my lack of success as a cricketer. Together with a former school friend, I had for two or three years been a spectator at the home matches of a club in a nearby town and as we were both now at work, we plucked up courage to apply for membership. Our subscriptions were accepted promptly enough but apart from being allowed to bowl our hearts out at evening net practice, the chance to demonstrate our prowess in a second-eleven match was denied us. Until that is, the local ironworks annual holiday depleted the team to such an extent that I was asked to make up the numbers in an away game. I batted at number eleven, had my stumps spread-eagled second ball, wasn't called upon to bowl, and spent the latter half of the afternoon miserably retrieving the ball from the nettle-infested fringes of the boundary.

Meanwhile, my daydreams were centred increasingly around Enid. Her fair image had made a disturbing impression on my mind ever since the morning when Bert Trouncer had performed what passed for introductions. I gained a warm feeling of reassurance on seeing her smart green-framed cycle leaning by her office wall; better still on watching from the survey office doorway as she elegantly dismounted and swept with a swirl of skirt indoors.

On one occasion, Lionel, all too aware of my infatuation and seemingly willing to assume the role of Cupid from the cherubic Bert, offered to let down one of her tyres to enable me to play the gallant and re-inflate it. Baffled by my confused reluctance, he threatened instead to remove the saddle and to tell Enid that I was the culprit. Cheeks aflame, I stormed back indoors and immersed myself even deeper into the inexhaustible depths of Box Five.

One afternoon, on my way back to the office tired and dishevelled after a day spent surface surveying around the boilers and gantries of the New Pit, I was confronted by a mirage, in the form of Enid. Mounted on her shining cycle, she rode into view and on reaching me, braked and began to chat as though we had known one another for an age. Gulping in disbelief, I searched my mind for something to say. Nothing came. Still Enid chatted on, her adorable ringing laugh making me tingle with delight. Suddenly she was gone. She hadn't seemed to notice my soot-smeared face, my shabby clothes, my dull, faltering speech. I floated back to the office through a glowing world of boundless promise.

Emboldened, I vowed to seize every opportunity to renew contact with this exquisite creature. I began to invent trivial errands in an attempt to confront her. I would take my courage in both hands and ask her out, come what may. To my chagrin however, days passed with no trace of Enid. The green cycle no longer adorned the office wall. Perhaps she was ill, or maybe on holiday. Or perhaps Mr. Degg was collecting her in his car. Yet I felt certain I had heard the faint clatter of her typewriter from behind the green door on one of my contrived prowls along the front of the buildings.

Then one morning, on hearing the slam of a car door, I peeped outside just in time to see an unfamiliar young woman wave to a departing car before disappearing through the green door. Lionel, hovering near, read my unhappy thoughts.

'Sad about Enid,' he remarked casually. 'Packed it in and gone to work in the shirt factory. Better money - and she won't have old Degg's wanderin' hands to bother about.' I cringed in misery, recalling something Enid had said at our meeting that had puzzled me ever since - something to the effect that she thought Mr. Elliston was a real gentleman, which was more than she could say of some people.

'And don't start getting any fancy ideas about the new typist,' Lionel added with a leer. "For one thing, she's married, and for another, she'd gobble you up for breakfast and then ask for more.'

*****************

I learned a fair amount about the new trainee, Desmond, long before he joined the staff. The son of a coal face worker at New Pit, he lived in the next street to Bert Trouncer, had gained a scholarship to the grammar school that I had been deemed unfit for, and was, according to Lionel, a prominent member of a highly successful youth football team that had won virtually everything winnable in local soccer for the past few years. It was with some apprehension, therefore, that I awaited the Monday morning in September on which my fellow trainee was to commence duty.

Desmond - Des to everyone, Mr. Elliston apart, from that first morning - took to the office routine like a duck to water. Neat featured, slightly built, and with no trace of the acne that had plagued me from the onset of puberty, he oozed a quick-witted confidence. This appealed to Lionel from the start, matching as it did his own temperament and providing scope for his own particular brand of racy humour that, with only Bert and me on whom to sharpen it, had hitherto been under-exploited.

Not that Bert was in any way left out. His yarns, often concerning characters known both to Lionel and Des, prompted either or both of the younger men to embellish them in his own fashion and in time, storytelling, increasingly of a lewd variety, gradually took over from singing as the background to our work.

50

But it was Des's knowledge of the complexity of mining itself that impressed me most. For whereas I, to my shame, was still trying to comprehend the basic processes and to master the baffling terminology used, this miner's son appeared to know everything there was to know about the underground world before he had even set foot on the cage.

I revealed my thoughts on this matter one day to Bert, who to my surprise embarked on a detailed account of his own background. He, like me, was a black sheep - the first of his family to go into mining. He had begun working on the estate in the old squire's time and had drifted into surveying almost by accident. Until nationalisation, together with his superior, Mr. Elliston, he had been responsible for all the surveying, both above and below ground, for the entire estate.

'There was no chance to qualify in those days,' he recalled, not without a trace of bitterness. 'Of course, Mr. Elliston had qualified during his time with one of the big companies. But I was stuck - no scope for promotion for me. There wasn't then and there isn't now.' Suddenly I saw a pathetic side to the amiable little man. But Bert was quick to rally. 'You'll be starting your day release at Nottingham soon,' he reminded me. 'Make the most of it.' My doubts must have been all too obvious to see. 'Do your best - you can't do more than that,' he said. 'And if you can't make it, remember there's another world waiting beyond Swainsbrook pit tip.'

*****************

Des and I travelled together by bus to Nottingham. The blue double-decker crawled through a string of drab colliery villages straddling the Derbyshire-Nottinghamshire border country and from our upper-deck seats we could see a rolling landscape of small hedged fields and scattered farms and woods, interspersed with mine tips, headstocks and tall smoking chimneys.

Almost empty at first, the bus gradually filled up with passengers, chiefly women and girls off to work in the city. To begin with, I was amazed at the cool, methodical way in which Des appraised the merits of the more attractive of these as they took their seats, scarcely lowering his voice as he commented, not only on their faces, but also on their figures.    Relishing my discomfort, he extended his assessment to include a form of grading, using his own five-point scale of desirability and digging me gleefully in the ribs whenever a girl placed at either end of the scale passed our seats.

'Ey, look at them legs - worth five. I wouldna' mind 'er,' followed a  little later by 'Bloody 'ell, what a mug she's got - not worth one, even.  You can 'ave 'er!'

Amongst the queue waiting to board at a windswept market place was a gangling youth with heavily creamed dark hair and the bristly beginnings of a moustache.  He and Des exchanged enthusiastic greetings:

'Ey up, Andy. Didna' know tha' went to th' Tech on Thursdays.'

'Ey up, Des.  Well, I guh t' Nottingham,' the youth paused for effect before adding ' - dunna allus end up at th' Tech, though.'

Andy slid into the seat behind and lit up a cigarette.  The packet was proffered in our direction and Des promptly accepted.  Andy, I soon discovered, was in his second year of a mining engineering course and the two had until recently played in the same all-conquering football team. His hint that the city held attractions other than his day - release course had aroused Des's curiosity. Andy however, was vague.

'There's pubs an' pictures an' lots o' shops,' he began, adding with an air of mystery, ' - an' wimmin.'

Des leered knowingly. 'Nottingham's full o' wimmin.'

Andy conceded the fact. 'Yeh, but you've got to know where t' look for th' sort o' wimmin I mean'

The topic turned to football as the bus crawled along the bustling streets into the heart of the city.

Appropriately enough, the mining department was situated in the basement of the massive stone-faced college buildings. Our day was a full one, with the morning session devoted to colliery surveying and geology, while mathematics and technical drawing occupied the afternoon. We had lunch in the college refectory and there was time for a brief tour of the nearby part of the city in the hour-long midday break.

To my relief, I was able to cope reasonably well with the morning timetable. Like me, the fifteen or so other trainees were also new to the theory of surveying and with no previous knowledge assumed, the pace was gentle. The geology I positively enjoyed. Maps and topographical literature had always held a fascination for me and thanks to a simple pocket guide to fossils, I already possessed a sketchy understanding of the subject and looked forward to making my own fossil collection from underground finds.

The afternoons were a different matter entirely. Many of the other students had already gained experience of technical drawing and on discovering this, the lecturer set off at a cracking pace, leaving me - and a handful of other unfortunates - behind, becalmed and bewildered.

But it was my inability in mathematics, with which the interminable afternoon session commenced, that caused me the greatest anguish. Alone it seemed among all the trainees, I appeared to lack even the most rudimentary understanding of the subject. The very mention of the words algebra and trigonometry struck dumb terror into my heart. I froze in panic, re-living the nightmare sessions with Father over my loathsome Hall and Knight school textbook. I peered at the blackboard through a fog of incomprehension, copied notes and formulae as though written in a foreign language, and rather than risk Father's offers of help, relied on cribbing sufficient homework during the lunch hour to prevent the depths of my inadequacy from being exposed.

From the outset I knew in my heart that this course of action was doomed to failure. Aptitude at maths was as essential to surveying as eyes were to seeing. Uneasily I recalled Mr. Wilkes's advice on the day of my interview; yet not only had I failed to enrol for extra maths but I was not even coping with its basic demands on my day-release course. And my sins would surely find me out, for my future as a trainee depended ultimately on successfully completing the first year of study .And that would be decided by examination in the following summer.

# Chapter 7

**F**ather's assurances that my work would be chiefly office-based soon began to take on a decidedly hollow ring. With three collieries to serve, Mr. Elliston's small team of surveyors were kept constantly busy; seldom did a day pass without either Bert or Lionel being underground, and more often than not, both Des and I would be called upon to assist them.

It was not long before I became acquainted with Oakfield Manor, which with Swainsbrook and Birch Park completed the trio of collieries within our sub-area. Although, like its neighbours, Oakfield Manor had operated originally as a shaft mine, the greater part of its output was obtained now by means of a tunnel, known as an adit, which had been driven at a gently dipping gradient into a wooded hillside on the western edge of the coalfield.

This long-established colliery was named after a 15th century fortified manor house, the crumbling remains of which stood nearby on the opposite bank of the little River Amber, dominating the landscape for miles around. As a boy, I had gazed with awe at this gaunt distant ruin from my bedroom window and had longed to visit it. Mother, however, had insisted that it was closed 'for the duration' - a phrase that for long puzzled me, and which, I suspect, came in useful to excuse her from having to take me there.

We travelled the three or so miles to and from the colliery by public service bus. This occasionally led to difficulties, for the bus was frequently crowded and the presence of three miners, loaded down with bulky equipment, did nothing to please the other passengers, especially on the return trip when our clothes were plastered with mud from the wet working conditions that were a feature of the adit's shallow workings.

On one such occasion, perched on the edge of the seat to avoid contact with the person alongside, I lost my balance as the bus lurched at a bend and the telescopic levelling staff I was holding flew from my hands to extend to its full ten-foot length along the gangway, narrowly missing the agitated conductor. Lionel and Des sat convulsed with laughter as I was given a lengthy rebuke on my irresponsible behaviour with 'That there ruler'.

****************

But it was down Swainsbrook New Pit that most of my early underground experience was gained, assisting Bert, together with Dan, his loyal and capable linesman. In time, I began to get used to my steel-capped boots and I had cause very early on to be thankful for my helmet, which saved me from serious injury. I was still finding it difficult to ride the conveyors. Leaping on to the moving rubber belt after my tackle was simple enough; my problem lay in getting off and retrieving it before it vanished into the distance. I usually followed the nimble little Bert, knowing that if for some reason I was unable to grab the equipment, he would do so for me. Once however, thinking I had mastered the technique, I rashly rode first and on nearing the loading point, delayed my jump and had to scramble in panic from the belt as it climbed to its delivery point, hitting my head on a girder and falling in a sprawling heap on the rocky floor. Luckily, my helmet bore the brunt of the impact and I got away with a severe headache, while the operator at the loader end was able to grab the legs as they were about to disappear into a tub of coal.

The one item of personal equipment I had yet to make use of was my knee- pads. I seemed to have walked for miles underground without once having had cause to kneel and after ruefully inspecting the sores behind my knees at shift end one day, I rashly raised the matter with Lionel.

'What - you mean to say you've not been on a face yet?' he exclaimed in wide-eyed disbelief. 'You skiving devil! We'll soon put that right. You'll think your pads are the best thing ever invented!' He was as good as his word. A few days later, together with my untried knee-pads, I was initiated into the mysteries of the coal face - the front line in the battle for coal - manned by the crack battalions of colliers. It was not until then that I began to appreciate that all other mine workers, including ourselves, were essentially a supporting unit to this army of fearless, highly-skilled men.

This particular face, the first of many I was to crawl along over the coming years, was in a four-foot thick seam, known as the low main, roughly a mile and a half from the New Pit shaft bottom. About a hundred and fifty yards long, it was served by three parallel roadways, known as gates, the middle one of which was the conveyor gate, along which the coal travelled towards the pit bottom. The two tail-gates, at either end of the face, served as airways and as supply routes, along the rails of which ponies drew tubs of timber supports.

Like the other local mines, Swainsbrook New Pit operated a three-shift system. Coal was extracted on the day shift, while the afternoon shift concentrated on undercutting and blasting, in preparation for the following day, as well as advancing the three gates. The night - shift men erected supports of blasted rock, known as packing, to counter subsidence, as well as dismantling and re-assembling the face conveyor, ready for the day shift to continue the process.

To say that I was ill-prepared for what awaited me that morning is something of an understatement. True, I had my pads, without which my knees would have been reduced to lumps of raw meat in minutes. But what I had failed to realise was that a coal face in a four-foot seam was essentially a one hundred and fifty yards-long tunnel, in which standing was impossible and in which twenty men, each working independently in his own stint, laboured for seven hours, equipped only with a pick, a long handled iron levering bar, a hammer and a shovel. And although the wall of coal had been undercut and loosened with explosive charges, every lump had to be loaded by shovel onto the face conveyor, which could only be done by kneeling with the legs apart and by swinging the shovel in a sideways motion, thus putting tremendous strain on the abdominal muscles.

But this was not all. As he began to clear his stint of coal, the collier had to set roof supports. These were wooden or metal props, which together with flat bars, also of wood or metal, were intended to prevent roof falls. Safety rules were rigorously applied by the officials, known as deputies, who patrolled the face, testing for gas, firing explosive charges where necessary, and exercising overall responsibility for their section of the mine.

I shall never forget the first time I watched a collier set a prop. Balancing the cylindrical length of timber - and the wedge, or lid, that was to be inserted between prop and roof - with one hand, he tapped the prop lightly into position with the other and then drove home the wedge with four or five cleanly struck two-handed hammer blows of tremendous power, leaving the prop absolutely vertical.

Compared with all this intense physical activity, our task - measuring the length of the face with a linen box-tape - was easy. Even so, crawling along a coal-littered rocky floor, avoiding loaded shovels, weaving between pit props, with primitive lamps; breathing coal dust and with ears assailed by crashing coal, scraping shovels and throbbing conveyor motors - all helped to make standing once more in the comparative comfort of a supply gate seem like a luxury.

It was no coincidence that my happiest times underground were those spent assisting Bert. However difficult the conditions and whatever the setbacks we encountered, he could always be relied upon to lift the spirits with his genial quips and harmless banter. He was known to almost all the men we met on our travels throughout the New Pit's extensive workings, not only as the surveyor - or dialler, as he was called by some of the older men - but also as a favourite comic turn in a local concert party. In addition, his services were in great demand for the drawing-up of plans for house extensions, garages and similar minor building works and it was common practice for an agreement for such work to be struck while on our rounds.

A good deal of our work underground involved the use of a dumpy level, an instrument rather like a telescope in appearance and mounted, like the dial, on a tripod. The standard joke among the older men was to pretend the level was a camera, and a group would pause in their work, remove their helmets, and pose with grinning blackened faces as Bert - with many a 'Smile please - watch the birdie!'- shone his light upon them from behind his instrument.

Another source of amusement involved the measuring staff on which Bert's dumpy level was focussed. As the staff-holder, my job was to illuminate it with my lamp and occasionally Bert would call for me to point at one particular section to help him take a reading. Normally I would use a pencil or possibly my finger for this purpose but if one of Bert's cronies happened to be nearby, he would invariably unbutton and apply part of his private anatomy to the staff, prompting a deprecatory response from the squinting Bert.

Snap-time provided Bert with the perfect opportunity to indulge to the full his gifts as a storyteller. Unlike Lionel - who believed in snatching a ten-minute break whenever and wherever the opportunity arose - Bert liked to partake of a leisurely meal in a carefully chosen place. Often this entailed trudging a considerable distance away from our working area - to an engine house, a quiet dust-free airway or a deputies' cabin, where we could make ourselves comfortable before doing justice to our picnic, as the little man insisted in calling it.

Often we would be joined at some stage in our snap break by a handful of other men - fitters, electricians, pump-men, haulage hands - who would squat down alongside us, with or without their own snap, for no other reason, it seemed to me, than to listen to Bert's stories. Unlike his vast repertoire of jokes, Bert's range of stories was a limited one, based more or less on incidents in his early life. But they were told with such comic skill that I never tired of listening, even though I had sat through the performance many times before.

As a youth, Bert had spent some time assisting an undertaker and a good number of his tales described his macabre experiences during that time. One which he never tired of telling concerned the difficulty he and his employer encountered in attempting to lift an incredibly stout farmer into his coffin. I had been told of this man's exceptional girth by my mother, who had witnessed the lengthy push-and-pull procedure needed to get him in and out of the car sent to fetch him to vote on election day; Bert's tale, though gruesome, was told with expansive mime and gesture that had his audience convulsed.

Another memorable undertaking yarn that offered ample scope for Bert's comic gifts concerned a hunchback. Lifting the rigid corpse into the coffin was easy enough; the problem was getting the lid down. To achieve this, the young Bert had been ordered to straddle the body, facing the feet, and to press the knees down while the undertaker applied his efforts to the hunchback's shoulders. Unknown to our hero, for some reason his superior relaxed his pressure and Bert, assuming that they had succeeded in their labours, glanced round to find the corpse apparently looking over his shoulder.

From undertaking, it was but a short step to the subject of ghosts, and here again Bert had sufficient colourful tales to keep us entertained for as long as we were prepared to listen. Two of his best stories concerned attempts made to frighten miners who had been forthright in denying the existence of ghosts. In the first of these, the sceptic was an elderly night-shift deputy, whose walk to work took him through a churchyard and who steadfastly ridiculed suggestions that he might one night encounter a ghost. To put his courage to the test, a workmate lay in wait for him in the churchyard one night, clad in a white sheet. At the old man's approach, the figure crouched down before a grave alongside the churchyard path, moaning ' I can't get in! I can't get in!' Instead of fleeing in fear, however, the old man set about the shrouded figure with his stick, shouting 'Can't get in, does tha' say? Why, tha's no bloody business bein' out!'

In the other story, a loud-mouthed young miner who boasted that, ghosts or no ghosts, nothing could prevent him from getting an uninterrupted night's sleep, was challenged to spend the night in an unoccupied house reputed to be haunted, which he promptly agreed to do. Meanwhile, those set on testing his resolve had ensured that creaking doors, rattling windows and various other sounds, guaranteed to frighten, would reduce him to a nervous wreck before daylight. At the appointed hour, the young man arrived at the house with his camp-bed and nightclothes, undressed and settled down to sleep, untroubled by the various sounds intended to ruin his repose. However, during the night, he woke to hear a ghostly voice whisper: 'There's only me - and thee!' This was too much for the braggart. Throwing off his covers, he leapt out of bed, screaming: 'Just let me get my boots on - and there'll only be thee!'

Not all Bert's stories were of a humorous nature. One in particular - which he insisted was authentic - concerned the mysterious disappearance of an under-manager some years earlier at a nearby colliery. According to Bert, work had ceased for the annual holiday and only three men - the under-manager, the winding-engine man and the banksman - were on duty. One morning, the under-manager went down the mine to carry out a routine inspection, telling the banksman to await his signal at a certain time, on hearing which he was to inform the winding -engine man to lower the cage for him to surface. The banksman waited but no bell was heard. Eventually a rescue party was summoned and an extensive search made. However, no trace of the missing official was ever found. Bert told his silent audience that to this day the incident remained a complete mystery, although one theory was that the under-manager had been in some kind of difficulty, and had bribed the banksman to say he had gone down the mine, whereas he had in fact fled the country.

An inevitable consequence of working with Bert was that the time we spent underground was often far longer than strictly necessary. Surveyors, unlike other workers, were not subject to the clocking-in system and consequently we were free to return to the surface once our task was completed. On the occasions when Lionel accompanied us, I was conscious of his ill-disguised impatience at these lengthy delays; he once hinted, half in jest, to Bert that perhaps the state of the little man's home life was such that he was in no hurry to return to it. The barb drew no response, however, and as usual we reached the pithead baths long after the other men had departed and showered in leisurely comfort.

## Chapter 8

After years of uninterrupted routine, changes were afoot at the survey office. It had long been apparent - at least to us - that we were seriously understaffed; this unsatisfactory state of affairs had at last been recognised in higher places and as a result the new year would see the personnel augmented by two new appointments - an additional surveyor and another trainee.

Mr. Elliston broke the news on one of the rare mornings that all four of us were in the office together. The sense of occasion gave rise to rather more nervous coughing than usual as he outlined the new method of working that would come into operation in a few months' time. We listened in silence, each considering how the changes would affect him personally as our superior, flushed and solemn, allocated our duties. As from January, each of the three collieries in the sub-area would be the responsibility of a senior member of staff, assisted by a trainee. The atmosphere intensified as Mr. Elliston went on. We learnt that Bert would be in charge of Swainsbrook, with David, the new trainee, as his assistant; Lionel would become responsible for Oakwood Manor, assisted by Des; and I would be assigned to Birch Park as assistant to the new surveyor, who was being transferred from area office.

I noticed Lionel and Des exchanging grins of relief. There would of course be occasions, Mr. Elliston continued, when staff would need to be flexible, and prepared to assist at collieries other than that to which they were attached. He went on to cover other, less- pressing consequences that would result from the new arrangements but our attention was straying long before he had finished. When he finally disappeared through his door, Lionel and Des went into an exuberant huddle. Bert caught my eye across the table.

'Remember - you were here first,' he said. 'The new man may be coming as your gaffer but you've got one advantage over him – at least you know the pit. If he's any sense he'll take that into consideration when he arrives.'

****************

I spent the next few days speculating which, if any, of the men I had met in the area office on the day of my interview would soon be my immediate superior. They had seemed an affable bunch, apart from the wizened little man with the indigestion and violent temper. What if........? I shuddered at the thought.

Mercifully, my fears were soon dispelled. Mr. Elliston called me into his office a few days later. A fair-haired, heavily built young man rose from a chair and extended his hand in greeting.

'Gordon, I'd like you to meet your new colleague who will be in charge at Birch Park in the new year,' Mr. Elliston said. 'This is Mr. Spencer.'

'Alf to you, Gordon.' The grin was easy, the eyes, set in the almost cherubic face, gave a ready twinkle. My relief was almost ecstatic.

We saw very little of Mr. Elliston as the year drew towards its end. As the new order - in the form of the National Coal Board - became firmly established, he was increasingly called away to meetings at area office, to which, not being a driver, he had to travel by bus. Occasionally, on the days when he was back in his own office, he would be visited by other officials of senior rank, who arrived in sleek cars, wearing smart suits and talking with smooth accents.

One such caller was the Area Chief Surveyor, Mr. Wilkes. He made a point of paying a brief visit to our office, where he chatted good- humouredly with Bert and Lionel and nodded distantly to Des and myself. I hovered uneasily, half- fearing that he would recall my interview and enquire whether I had enrolled for an evening maths course, but my anxiety proved unnecessary; obviously he had more important matters on his mind.

After he had gone, Lionel somewhat shamefacedly held aloft a couple of tickets.

'Cost me five bob, that little chat', he announced ruefully. 'Just asked old Wilkes how rehearsals for his new play are going and he promptly flogged me these.' Bert gave one of his rich chuckles.

'Serves you right for trying to make a good impression - he'll have you on the stage yet if you're not careful.'

Theatrical matters had for some time been a subject of good-natured disagreement between the two. As a seasoned concert-party performer, Bert had always expressed contempt for actors in amateur dramatics, who he seemed to regard as affected and snobbish. Lionel, however, had recently begun courting a former grammar- school girl, said to be devoted to all aspects of the arts, and was trying hard to please her. Pauline's father, a deputy at New Pit, was a devout Baptist and pillar of the local chapel and Bert - mischievous as ever - went on to warn Lionel of the dangers inherent in taking his daughter to see this particular play, which was said to contain rather daring scenes of a sexual nature. Lionel, for once uncomfortable at having his love-life discussed so flippantly in front of two impressionable trainees, sought to laugh the matter off.

'Don't worry - me and Pauline have nothing to learn from a play,' he scoffed. 'Wilkes and his leading lady should see us in action in her front room – they'd learn something, that's for sure'. But Bert had heard enough.

'Aye - and Pauline's dad would too, I fancy,' he muttered dryly, resuming his work.

Mr. Elliston's fondness for gadgets was almost an obsession. Seldom did a week pass without him bringing some novelty or other into the office for us to see, examine and where possible, experiment with. His specialities were office sundries - pens, inks, adhesives, miscellaneous clips, tapes, sharpeners - in fact anything new that caught his eye. He was especially prone to newspaper advertisements and sent away for any manner of new lines, more it seemed out of curiosity than for any other reason, and his delight at putting his latest acquisitions through their paces - with us as an appreciative audience -was almost childlike.

On one occasion, noticing that Bert was suffering from a persistent facial rash, he insisted on lending him a new-fangled safety razor on an extended trial. The rash disappeared soon afterwards - of its own accord Bert told us, as he had never shaved with the razor - but Mr. Elliston expressed his delight at the success of his novelty and was heard telling others of its effectiveness, quoting Bert as a highly satisfied user.

Being one of what Bert called ' The old school', whose working career had spanned difficult times, Mr. Elliston found some aspects of the new order hard to adjust to. Having had to struggle along, making do with limited resources, he was sorely distressed at the amount of waste that the new generation regarded as normal. To Lionel's ill-concealed annoyance, he was in the habit of removing off-cut scraps from wastepaper baskets, sharpening pencils until they virtually disappeared and trying to practise other economies that to the exasperated younger man appeared petty and penny-pinching.

*****************

But it was the matter of the Nadelverb that came nearest to causing a rift between the two men. On one of his now frequent visits to area headquarters, Mr Elliston had met a young surveyor who while on military service in Germany had acquired by some means an unusual type of theodolite once used in the Ruhr coalfield. Mr Elliston, naturally enough, had expressed interest in this instrument and its owner had brought it over and left it for him to examine at his leisure.

The first we knew of it was when the office outer door burst open one winter afternoon and an excited Mr Elliston invited us to come outside and inspect his latest novelty. The unfamiliar theodolite had been set up on its special tripod near the Old Pit winding-engine house and we were asked to gather round for a demonstration of its apparently unique and highly sophisticated features.

It so happened that our superior had chosen a bitterly cold day for this exercise, and although he was suitably clad to withstand the wind's icy blast, in his enthusiasm he had completely overlooked the fact that we had come straight from our heated office with no time to don our coats. Oblivious to our shivers and stamping feet, Mr Elliston launched into a detailed explanation of the workings of the instrument, after which first Bert, then Lionel, was invited to take sightings of nearby objects. By the time that we were back indoors, thawing ourselves out in front of the antiquated stove, it was unanimously agreed that, given our way, the Nadelverb would have been permanently entombed down its German coal-mine.

Rashly, we had assumed that we had seen the last of the Nadelverb, but that was far from the case. A few days later, as we were busily engaged in trying to complete the inevitable backlog of office work before the Christmas holiday, Mr Elliston dropped a bombshell. He had arranged for us all - himself included - to descend the Old Pit on the following afternoon to try out the Nadelverb in underground conditions before its owner called to collect it.

The silence that greeted this announcement was both long and sombre. We were dismayed. Barely a fortnight to Christmas and enough work to last us through to the new year. Despairing glances were exchanged but no-one spoke. Sensing that his news had met with something of a muted welcome, Mr Elliston attempted to soften the blow. He pointed out that apart from himself, Bert was the only one of us who had had the opportunity to descend the Old Pit. It was, he went on, one of the oldest mines in the county and its famous eight-foot thick top hard seam had, until its exhaustion, provided coal for some of the most prominent families in the land. The descent would be a valuable experience for younger colleagues – perhaps our one and only opportunity to see for ourselves what was essentially a Victorian coal mine, happily preserved until the present day.

The flood gates burst the moment the door closed. Lionel was beside himself with impotent rage. He was taking Pauline to see the play at the miners' welfare the following evening and had been invited round to her house for tea beforehand - his first opportunity to get his feet under the table.

'Him and his new toys!' he fumed. 'Just like an overgrown kid - as though we've nothing to do but –.' His indignation choked him to a standstill.

'Why can't we go down in th' mornin', instead?' Des demanded, turning to Bert. The little man grimaced.

'It takes ages to get steam up for that old winding engine,' came the reply. '- and in any case, an overman has to carry out an inspection beforehand. It all has to be arranged to suit the management - not us.'

I kept silent. I had no appointments to keep. One day was pretty much like the next as far as I was concerned. And I had heard that the top hard seam was exceptionally rich in fossils.................

An eventful day had one more surprise in store. As we mounted our bikes in the failing afternoon light, Des called across to me. 'It's our youth club Christmas party on Friday night an' we can invite a friend - would tha' like to come?'

'Yes, Des - yes, please!' I gulped in grateful disbelief, and pedalled happily homeward in the gathering gloom.

# Chapter 9

**O**ur descent of the Old Pit was scheduled for two o'clock but as Bert had predicted, getting up sufficient steam was a time-consuming operation and it was nearer half-past before the five of us, complete with Nadelverb, were able to crowd on to the tiny cage. We were wound down at a speed that seemed hardly quicker than that of a department store lift, the difference being that our descent was accompanied by a sound of rushing water - evidence of the need for the continuous pumping that took place in the waterlogged abandoned workings.

Mr. Bartlett, the elderly overman who was to accompany us, was waiting in the pit bottom, having made his way through the labyrinth of old levels from the workings of the main colliery. He and Mr. Elliston clearly held one another in high regard and formal introductions, handshakes and polite conversation ensued in the damp and musty shaft bottom, lit only by the light from our lamps.

I had assumed that we would be Nadelverbing - as Lionel and Des had called the previous day's exercise - close to the pit bottom. But Mr. Elliston had other ideas. In order to put the instrument through its paces, he explained, it would be necessary to set it up on or near a steep gradient, where its full potential could be assessed. There followed a lengthy consultation between Mr. Bartlett and Bert - who knew the old workings well - before a suitable location was agreed on. Lionel, meanwhile, was already taking anxious glances at his watch and muttering darkly to Des about the futility of the enterprise.

We had walked only a short distance along what had once been the main haulage roadway when Mr. Elliston, who together with Mr. Bartlett was leading, brought us to a halt. At this point, he announced, we would make a short diversion to see the only accessible section of the famous top hard seam, which was exposed nearby. Even Lionel was impressed by the sight that soon met our lamps. Here, glistening before us, was a solid wall of coal, twice as thick as the deep seams that were now being worked. There was no need for knee-pads here, as someone remarked. At Mr. Elliston's prompting, the overman gave a brief history of the mining of this celebrated seam; how it had been used to heat some of the finest stately homes in the land and had brought fame and prosperity to the Playfair-Westwood family. At this point Lionel added his own whispered observation to Des, which judging by the stifled guffaw it produced, had something to do with the squire's lady-killing exploits.

The place chosen for Nadelverbing was a junction of two roadways, from which a steep incline, known as a stone-head, had been driven from the top hard to strike another seam called the deep soft. Accompanied by Mr. Bartlett, I was despatched to suspend a flame lamp some distance down the stone- head. As we descended, the overman shone his beam along the roof supports to reveal what proved to be the finest example of timbering I was privileged to see in my ten years underground. Extending as far as the beam penetrated, these timbers, consisting of two uprights, supporting two diagonals and topped by a horizontal bar, had been set with such precision and had been so perfectly preserved for over fifty years that the effect was almost architectural. Yet here they were, sealed away from view in the darkness of an abandoned coal mine, and known only to a handful of ageing colliery officials.

We reached the point at which the lamp was to be suspended and that done, turned off our electric lamps and waited in the flame lamp's dull glow for the signal to return. My expressed admiration for the timbering prompted Mr. Bartlett to tell me more about the history of the Old Pit and this led in turn to talk of fossils. The overman confirmed my belief that the top hard had yielded many examples but assured me that the most remarkable fossil bed lay in the deep soft seam, and consisted of the remains of the small brachiopod lingula mytiloides. He offered, subject to Mr. Elliston's agreement, to show me this remarkable geological feature and volunteered to broach the subject at the earliest opportunity.

Receiving the awaited signal, we set off on the return climb. I had assumed that the greater part of the exercise had been completed during our absence but that proved to be far from the case. We arrived to find Mr. Elliston and Bert poring intently over the Nadelverb and Lionel pacing to and fro like a father-to-be outside a maternity ward.

'Four o'clock and they're still at it!' he fumed to Des, who, like me, had just returned with a lamp. 'Some of us have homes to go to and better things to do than play with fancy toys down a bloody pit.'

Almost another hour was to pass - with first Mr. Bartlett, then a tight-lipped Lionel, and finally Des and me invited to learn something of the Nadelverb's mysteries - before we at last set off for the waiting cage. Back on the surface once more, we carried the equipment back to the office and led by an almost frantic Lionel, prepared to disperse - Mr. Elliston to his private ablutions, the rest of us on our bikes to the pit-head baths.

I was just about to follow the others into the darkness when Mr. Elliston called me back. 'Mr. Bartlett tells me that you'd like to see our famous fossil bed,' he said. 'I've told him you may go one day early in the new year. I'm so pleased that you are taking so much interest in the work. Keep it up!'

I thanked him and bade him good afternoon. Could an interest in geology possibly help compensate for my failings in other aspects of my course? I would know for certain by next summer but it was hard even now to avoid reading the writing on the wall.

*****************

The youth club was held in the schoolroom of a chapel in the next village. On hearing of my intentions, Mother gave a sniff of disapproval; long-lapsed C of E. herself, she regarded all nonconformists with a kind of grim amusement and what went on in their ugly little brick chapels as vaguely distasteful.

'Shouldn't have thought that sort of thing would have been in your line,' she commented dryly. I pointed out that I was going as a guest to a party - nothing more than that. Mother was far from convinced; she sensed a trap.

'Even so, I should just watch out. I expect they're after new members. They'll be having you in if you're not careful.' The seeds of suspicion firmly planted, she switched to her indifferent mode. 'Anyway - please yourself. I expect you will in any case,' she said, turning away.

Des was waiting by the bus stop near to the side-street leading to the chapel. Groups - some of girls, others of youths - were turning under the one street lamp; laughter and suppressed excitement filled the air. My natural diffidence, reinforced by Mother's antagonism, gave way to a heady feeling of anticipation. As we too turned down the side-street, I was vaguely aware of two female forms, merged almost in the intimacy of shared giggling, lingering coyly ahead and peering behind at intervals. I remained utterly baffled why Des - with the world as I knew it at his feet - had invited me to partake of its delights. Baffled, yet eager to seize the chance that he had so unexpectedly offered.

We joined the buffeting, animated crowd in the schoolroom entrance. Youths were hanging up their coats on the rows of hat- pegs lining the wall. Groups of girls drifted in and out of a nearby cloakroom, from which an intoxicating whiff of scent spread its allure. Des was exchanging breezy 'Ey ups' with youths and girls on either side. I looked on enviously. Eventually, we were swept by the bantering tide into the spacious schoolroom. Wooden chairs, arranged in a wide circle, were already filling up rapidly. Des propelled me towards a couple of vacant seats alongside two girls, who giggled a greeting and launched into a rapturous account of Des's performance in the most recent football match. Taking this lavish praise in his stride, Des told them to be sure to attend the following day's match, a local derby with considerable prestige at stake. They assured him that they'd be there, come what may. Meanwhile, I waited in vain for some kind of introduction but none came. The girl furthest from me enquired of Des whether I was a footballer too.

'Nah - 'e plays a bit o' cricket - or so 'e reckons,' came the reply.

'I think cricket's boring,' she retorted. I sank into my chair, cheeks tingling.

A small, red-faced man stepped into the circle and clapped his hands for quiet. He introduced himself as the club leader and welcomed those of us who were present as guests. Before we made a start, he beamed, he must insist that the single-sex groups were broken up. We were to mix; the coloured paper hats that his wife was about to bring round would only be given to those sitting next to someone of the opposite sex. There followed a frantic swapping of seats, led, it seemed, by Des, who unceremoniously ejected the furthest of the two girls. She in turn commanded me to move over into Des's seat to make room for her in mine. Breathless, more through excitement than exertion, we settled into our new places.

Still smarting from her damning verdict on the game I revered, I searched desperately for some topic on which to venture a remark to the girl by my side. Before I could hit upon anything vaguely appropriate however, she was chattering animatedly to the youth on her other side. When I did finally manage to open my mouth it was merely to offer thanks to the lady dispensing the paper hats. My evening had not exactly got off to the best of starts.

As time passed, however, and the games compelled us to mingle, my self-consciousness finally loosened and I began to enjoy myself. From such static routines as ring-on-the-string and passing-the-parcel, we moved on to various team and novelty games. In one of these I encountered a youth who worked in the fitting shop at Swainsbrook. In the lull that preceded the refreshment break, we met again in the toilets. He expressed surprise at seeing me at the club. Hearing how I came to be there, he gave a knowing grin.

'Des wants t' find somebody to go out wi' Joan Shawcroft,' he said. ' 'E asked me - no fear!' He could see I needed further enlightenment. 'She's pally wi' Josie Slack - too pally for Des's likin' - an' 'e can't get Josie t' 'issen wi' Joan 'angin' around.'

The message got through to me at last. I could picture Mother's I-told-you-so look and almost hear her: 'You wouldn't listen to me. Think you know best.' It wasn't so much that I resented the way that Des had tried to use me; the girl - Joan - was attractive enough as far as I was concerned - but I sensed already that my chances with her - hidden as I undoubtedly was under Des's shadow - were slender in the extreme. What could I - an unsuccessful cricketer - offer to a girl whose bosom friend was associating with an accomplished footballer?

Des sidled over to me during refreshments. I detected a sheepish look in his eye.

'Joan wants t' know what she's done wrong,' he said out of

the side of his mouth. I blushed. 'Wrong? Why - nothing,' I stammered.

'Well, she seems t' think so,' came the reply. 'Come on over. She wants t' talk t' ya.' Dumbly, I followed him as he wove his way through the munching crowd. The two girls were whispering intently but broke off as we approached. Apprehensively, I stole a look at Joan; from the expression clouding her pretty blonde features, I read that the last thing she wanted just then was to talk to me.

Des had arranged that we were to see the girls to their bus stop before I caught my bus home. I was just about to follow them through the door when the club leader came over.

'Hope you've enjoyed the party,' he said. 'You're welcome to become a member. We meet again on the first Friday in the new year.' I thanked him. 'Oh, and as you probably know, we're having a club holiday at Morecambe in August - if you're interested,' he added.

Exchanging whispered giggles, Des and Josie led the way to the bus stop. As we passed beneath the corner lamp once more, I noticed he had his arm around her waist. Joan and I followed, the silence separating us as tangible as the garden walls on either side of the dimly-lit road. As the bus lights receded into the distance and we turned to go, Des gave me a playful nudge of the elbow.

'We're doin' well wi' them two,' he grinned. 'Yours – Joan -'s a bit o' alright - wouldna' mind 'er mesen.' As we neared my bus stop, he added, 'You'll join after Christmas if you've any sense. I know Joan's 'opin' y' will.'

The back door was locked when I reached home and it took several knocks before Mother finally opened it.

'What time do you call this?' she demanded as I entered.

'It's only half past ten. It didn't finish 'till ten.'

'Umph - so you stuck it out 'till the end, then. I thought you'd have had enough before then. Don't forget you're at work tomorrow morning.'

I knew at that moment that if I didn't utter, there and then, the words I had been rehearsing over and over again on the way home, I would never do so.

'It was the best party I've ever been to,' I blurted defiantly. '- and I'm joining the club when it starts again after Christmas. And I want to go with them to Morecambe for a week in August.' With that, breathless and still amazed at what I had said, I bid goodnight and climbed the stairs to bed.

# Chapter 10

Come what may, 1948 was to be a significant year. The exams I faced in June would decide my future as a trainee mine surveyor, while I was determined to renew my attempt to make my mark at cricket. As for affairs of the heart, I felt that my intended membership of the youth club, together with the prospect of a week at the seaside, would surely open up exciting new possibilities that hitherto had failed to come my way.

With the sub-area staff now increased to six, space was at a premium in the office. On the rare days when we were all office based, this caused difficulties; there simply wasn't room for everyone to work and this led to the need to plan underground tasks well in advance to ease the space problem.

I got on quite well with Alf Spencer, which was fortunate, as Bert now had the new trainee, David, under his wing and most of my time would now be spent assisting Alf with work relating to Birch Park. Like Lionel, Alf was to take his qualifying exam in the summer and his energies were directed somewhat single-mindedly towards that objective. This gave me the opportunity to play a far greater part in the day-to-day work than previously, which in turn helped to increase my confidence.

Alf had been a trainee in pre-nationalisation days but had left to join the army. He had not intended resuming his surveying career but like so many of us, had been persuaded that mining now offered fresh opportunities at the outset of what we were told was a new beginning. Pit work, I soon discovered, was to Alf the least appealing aspect of mine surveying. Unlike Lionel, for whom a shift underground meant more often than not an early finish to the day; or Bert, who was happy to work a full shift at a steady pace, with a sociable 'picnic' thrown in, Alf was at his happiest in a settled office routine. Like me, he had no miners in his family and being heavily-built and hence lacking the nimbleness of men from mining stock, he found the low roadways and difficult conditions at Birch Park irksome. In fact, I sensed that he had serious misgivings about having returned to mining but as he had recently married and set up home locally, he was determined to make a go of it.

As Alf didn't cycle and the staff car we had formerly had use of was no longer available, we had to walk the mile or so from our base to Birch Park. It was a pleasant enough walk, even with our cumbersome tackle, as it was chiefly along footpaths through fields. Alf had travelled widely during his army service and I listened with wonder to the tales he told, many of which, I soon realised, were spiced up for my benefit. As we got to know one another better, I confessed to Alf how difficult I found much of my day-release course and this led to an unburdening of the unsuccessful struggle I had had with my parents to become a journalist.

Alf listened with growing incredulity .How I could have allowed myself to be pushed into a career for which I was utterly unsuited was beyond his comprehension.

'You should have stood up to 'em,' he said. 'That's what I did. I wasn't having my old folks telling me how to live my life.' The army, he insisted, had opened his eyes and expanded his horizons. True, he was back in the pit for the time being, but it wouldn't be for long - he'd see to that. Turning his attention to my case, he went on to remind me that there were such things as correspondence courses. It was possible to study a whole range of subjects at home; no doubt journalism was one. It would mean a hard slog, studying after a day's work, but surely that was a price worth paying.

'As it is,' he said, 'you're a square peg. Do you really want to spend your life stuck in a bloody round hole?'

Mr Bartlett took me to see the fossil bed early in the new year. Armed with my virtually untried geologist's hammer and with my newly-issued lamp battery on my belt and spot-lamp on my helmet, I followed the elderly overman through the long-abandoned workings of the deep soft seam. As in the top hard, the roadways were in amazingly good condition, compared with the crushed and contorted girders of many of the more recent workings. Both seams had been worked by the ancient pillar-and-stall method, in which groups of men, under the direction of a senior miner known as a butty, worked as a self-contained unit in their stall, which was separated from its neighbour by a pillar of unworked coal. Now regarded as uneconomical, this way of extraction had the virtue of maintaining the workings in good order and of keeping surface subsidence to a minimum.

Mr Bartlett, I discovered, was not simply a miner, but something of a geologist and a historian too. As a young man, studying to qualify as an official had whetted his appetite for learning. He had enrolled for WEA courses in every conceivable subject over the years, but with special emphasis on geography and history. He had considered trying to enter one of the professions, such as teaching, but times were hard and with a young family to support, had had to resign himself to restricting his academic leanings to his leisure time. Not a trace of bitterness, regret even, emerged from his reflections as we picked our way through the abandoned workings. He had had a good life, he considered, and his approaching retirement would be happily filled, thanks to his grandchildren, his allotment and his bookshelf.

We reached the fossil bed at last. By the combined light of our lamps I could see in the rock above our heads a vast cluster of the tiny fossilised bivalve shells of the brachiopod lingula mytiloides and with difficulty managed to extract a few examples to add to my collection. Back at the office, I showed my finds to Mr Elliston and referred in passing to my conversation with Mr Bartlett and to the impression he had made on me.

'Did he tell you how he turned a serious injury into an advantage?' my superior enquired. At my puzzled response, he explained that following a severe injury to his writing hand, the overman had taught himself to write with the other. Fortunately the damaged hand had made a complete recovery, with the result that he was now ambidextrous.

\*\*\*\*\*\*\*\*\*\*\*\*\*\*\*\*\*

As the year advanced, the conflicting aspirations that had plagued me ever since my first day at work, intensified. On the one hand, men like Mr Elliston and Mr Bartlett won my respect and admiration for their dignity and quiet scholarship. On the other, I desperately craved acceptance among my peers and was prepared if necessary to go to absurd lengths to win, if not exactly their friendship, then at least their tolerance.

Nowhere did this dilemma manifest itself more than over my day-release course at Nottingham. We were only a few weeks into the new term when Des - who later said that he had calculated how many of the afternoon sessions he could afford to miss, yet still cover enough of the syllabus to scrape through the exams - failed to return one day after lunch. There was no afternoon registration and his absence did not appear to be noticed. He had been in the habit of disengaging from our regular group to meet his former football team mate, Andy, only to rejoin us later. On this occasion however, the two turned up at the bus stop and after Andy alighted, Des slid into the empty seat alongside mine.

'Tha' should a' bin wi' us this afternoon,' he grinned. 'Went t' th' pictures - ya want t' come wi' us next time.'

The next time arose a few weeks later. I had dreaded

being invited to join them, yet was painfully aware that faced with a decision, I would give in. What have you to lose? an ever more insistent inner voice seemed to say. You've as good as failed already. And so, for the first of several afternoons, I sat uneasily under the spell of the flickering screen, alongside two carefree truants, puffing contentedly on their Woodbines and discussing in matter-of-fact tones the physical attributes of every actress projected before us.

My attendance at the youth club, meanwhile, had not exactly had the effect that Des had intended. After a couple more strained and uncomfortable attempts at escorting Joan - in the company of Des and Josie - to the bus stop, I was relieved to see another youth usurp my ill-fitting role at the next meeting. By this time, I had formed a loose friendship with a small group of other youths, and their ready acceptance provided me with the reassurance I so badly needed.

\*\*\*\*\*\*\*\*\*\*\*\*\*\*\*\*

To my surprise, my outburst at Mother following the youth club Christmas party didn't produce the after- effects I feared. My Friday evenings out seemed to be accepted, albeit with silent resignation. So that when, in response to Father's question, I revealed that one of the youths in my little circle worked in a building society office and another for the county council, I sensed that any lingering opposition had been virtually dispelled. This was confirmed soon afterwards when Mother raised the subject of the forthcoming holiday.

'You'll need some new shirts if you're going to Morecambe,' she announced. 'Though from what I can recall of it from when your Father and I were there years ago, it wasn't a patch on Blackpool.'

If I needed any further incentive to pursue my aim to succeed at cricket, the Australians provided it. Led by the legendary Don Bradman, making his farewell tour, they were a formidable team, packed with talented personalities whose names were soon on everyone's lips as they set about the humiliation of the home side. Taking as my role model the man who had become every young cricketer's hero, Keith Miller, I transferred my allegiance from the club to which I had formerly belonged to the miners' welfare club. Here, I reasoned, my ability would surely be recognised. After all, I had based my style on that of the brilliant Miller himself - fast bowler and fearless big-hitting batsman. I'd even cultivated the appropriate mannerism - that of flicking back my unruly lock of hair after hurtling down an extra speedy delivery or after despatching with debonair ease another ball to the boundary. True, these heroics were accomplished on our back yard, using an undersized bat, a bald tennis ball, and a wicket chalked on Father's workshop door; but surely all this potential would soon win the recognition it deserved.

I soon discovered that other young hopefuls harboured similar ambitions. Youths of every shape, size and style were literally queuing up at evening net practice, eager to demonstrate their skills to the handful of astute and solemn committee men, former players themselves, who watched us with set jaws and sunken expressionless features and who occasionally drifted together in frowning huddles just beyond our earshot.

The limitations of my batting prowess were soon exposed. One evening, after I had ruefully repaired my shattered stumps for the third time in four balls, one of these exalted beings shuffled over and proffered a few well-chosen words of advice.

'Tha'll never mek a batter, lad,' he said, nodding sagely. 'Stick t' tha' bowlin' - but dunna try t' bowl suh fast - tha'll be knackered after a couple o' overs at th' rate tha' guz at it.'

Sobered, yet grateful for a crumb of recognition, I resolved to take this advice to heart; at least I had not been told that I wouldn't make a bowler. In fact, it took two or three games with the second eleven - during which my innocuous medium-pace bowling was gleefully plundered by a series of raw-boned young men employing virtually every stroke not to be found in the batsmanship manuals - to convince the selectors that like my batting, my bowling was something they could happily manage without.

By now it was June, and soon I would face a more severe and significant test. In this too, as I well knew, I would most likely be found wanting.

# Chapter 11

The first anniversary of my commencement at the survey office would have passed unnoticed but for Mr Elliston. True to his word, he had started bringing me Neville Cardus's accounts of the Australians' matches, clipped from *The Manchester Guardian*, and remarked one morning that a year had gone by since I joined his staff.

With the make-or-break examinations looming, I began to dread these encounters. The guilt I felt at absenting myself from some of the afternoon sessions at Nottingham was bad enough; how on earth would I be able to face this kindly, trusting and principled man when the truth was out and my abject failure to live up to the standard he had so unstintingly set for me was revealed?

From what I had heard from other trainees on the day-release course, Mr Elliston was totally unlike any other sub-area surveyor in the entire coalfield. He stood out as a lone survivor of an order that had almost completely disappeared, men of unswerving loyalty and integrity, whose pride and purpose lay in work well done. Status symbols - all forms of material wealth or ostentation - were utterly foreign to him. He had his pride, of course, and his contempt for the arrogant and pretentious, though controlled, was scathing. He led his team by example and the fact that many of us, for various reasons, failed to live up to his example was a reflection of our limitations, not his.

Typical of his kindness and consideration was the way in which he readily agreed to Des and me taking a week of our fortnight's leave entitlement together to accompany the youth club to Morecambe. August was the month during which the collieries closed for the annual holiday, thus providing surveyors with the chance to carry out their work without the usual interruption. Mr Elliston, however, pleased that two of his trainees were members of a chapel-based organisation, waived the rules on staggered leave and wished us well.

For my part, the year had passed quickly. Despite my early dismay at donning pit clothes and having to struggle with bulky equipment through unpleasant conditions underground, I had come to terms with this new life in a way I would never have thought possible. Thanks largely to Bert, I had gradually begun to see miners, not as a grey anonymous race existing on a different plane, but as individuals, each with his own personality that somehow transcended the bleak underground world we shared.

Alf Spencer, however, saw things differently. Born and bred among mining folk, though not from their background, he seemed to regard pit work as a dehumanising process, one which subjugated and degraded the personality. His army life - which he insisted had broadened his outlook - seemed also to have left him with a wariness, distaste even, not only for work underground but also for those toiling alongside us. Similarly thinking minds were not hard to find. Alf soon struck up an acquaintance with an elderly safety officer, a self-proclaimed lifelong Tory, who was openly contemptuous not only of nationalisation, which had provided him with a comfortable and well-paid job, but also of the government and of the miners themselves. This particular man never tired of telling us how his son, a grammar school scholarship boy, had left university with a first-class degree; held a prestigious position in London, and to his father's bewilderment, was a passionate Labour supporter.

There were times when Alf's biting sarcasm succeeded in alienating those we encountered underground. Once, as he was busily setting up the dumpy level in a stone- head, the group of miners snapping nearby struck up the familiar family-photograph pose and asked Alf to oblige.

'No time for comics today,' was the terse response, which caused a few of the men, unaccustomed to the new surveyor's sense of humour, to take offence and mutter a few uncharitable remarks in reply. Some time later, when we had cause to return to that part of the pit, I met with an uncharacteristically cool response as I greeted the men. Later, instead of waiting patiently with lamps averted as Alf began taking sightings, they carried on working as normal, passing to and fro in front of the instrument and making Alf's task increasingly difficult. Suddenly, as a couple of men passed carrying a steel girder, there was an outburst of rage from Alf. Somehow the girder had made contact with the tripod, knocking it off balance. But for Alf's timely action, the instrument would have crashed to the floor with disastrous results. The men's protests of innocence fooled nobody and Alf, realising that his curses fell on deaf ears, had no option but to start work all over again, to a background of suppressed laughter from his tormentors.

I pondered for some time on the reasons for Alf's aversion to the underground part of our work. Being tall and heavily built, he found the low, badly crushed roadways extremely hard to travel and even with our newly-issued cap lamps, which freed one hand, our bulky equipment made long journeys especially exhausting. There was more to Alf's aversion than this, however, and it soon became apparent that its chief cause was fear. Indeed, fear - of roof falls, explosions, poisonous gas, water inundation - was a spectre that lurked in the mind of everyone working underground. But as long as this fear was confined to the back of the mind, it could do little harm; in fact its presence there promoted an awareness of possible danger that acted as a form of safety mechanism. In Alf's case, however, fear stalked in the forefront of the mind. The least tiny trickle of rock particles from the roof caused him to jump; the rumble of a distant gob fall made his head jerk in instant panic. He took to walking between Colin, the linesman, and me and if for some reason I fell a few yards behind, he would bark an order to Colin to wait and refuse to move again until I had caught up.

Once, my cap-lamp having picked out what looked like a fossil in the roof, I paused to examine it more closely. Alf, meanwhile, realising that I was no longer immediately behind, bawled at me to hurry and on being given the reason for my delay, refused to listen and accused me of endangering our lives by trying to hack the specimen from the roof.

As it happened, I was not present to witness the sternest test of Alf's nerve. A roof fall on the afternoon shift had resulted in a fatality and measurements had to be taken at the scene for the drawing-up of plans for the inquest. Mr Elliston decided that I was too young and inexperienced to assist in this distressing task and Lionel was instructed to accompany Alf. The accident had occurred on a Friday afternoon and even though it was Monday morning when I next saw Alf, his face was still haggard and his eyes downcast. Lionel, by contrast, made light of the affair, giving Des and myself a gory account of what had taken place and joking about having found the unfortunate man's dentures near the fatal spot.

How would I have coped, I asked myself, had I been called upon to attend the tragic business? Pit accidents, as I well knew, were all too common, though thankfully fatalities were comparatively rare. However severe, the surveyor's job was to visit the site and take the necessary particulars. Far from reacting like Lionel, I would certainly have been affected in the way that Alf, for all his man-of-the-world manner, had been. For although I was coping - just about - with the daily routine, such a situation would have exposed me for what, in Alf's words, I knew myself to be - a square peg.

\*\*\*\*\*\*\*\*\*\*\*\*\*\*\*\*\*

As the exams approached, I willed myself to revise. I spent sweet summer evenings ploughing with a heavy heart through pages of notes, diagrams and formulae, making a futile gesture, as though mere hours devoted to self-inflicted misery would somehow count in my favour when the time came. Even Des, I noticed, was spurred into action; I overheard him picking Lionel's brains, posing questions and receiving answers that to me were virtually incomprehensible. As a last desperate resort, I directed my efforts single-mindedly towards geology - at least I would ensure that some marks, somehow, would be credited to my name.

The standard of the papers, when finally placed before me, were neither easier nor more difficult than I had anticipated. The surveying theory I could cope with in parts; the geology presented little difficulty; while the technical drawing I found hard going. As for the mathematics paper, it took one glance to confirm my utter inability to answer a single question. The results, we were told, would be announced by early August; in other words, before Morecambe. Six weeks to wait for official confirmation of what I knew already. Sooner or later I would have some serious thinking to do - and the sooner, it seemed to me, the better.

The opportunity was to come quicker than I expected.

## Chapter 12

I enjoyed surface work. I had long since learned to accept the fact that collieries were dirty places, where dust, water, oil, slime and discarded rubbish of every imaginable kind mixed together to produce a disgusting miasma of clogging filth and pervading stench. In this environment, inhabited only by persistent, soot-encrusted weeds and brazen, blackened starlings, laboured a motley crew of semi-skilled men known collectively as surface workers. Many of these, I discovered, had once been lusty young colliers, earning good money and enjoying health to match. But coal had exacted its price, and now - limping, bent and wheezy - they eked out a living sweeping screens, tipping waste, oiling axles and discharging countless other demeaning tasks in what passed for the open air. Out in all weathers, these shuffling, broken men, with their blackened claws and their bowed shoulders wrapped in sacking, comprised the mining underclass, for whom the new deal of nationalisation meant little, other than the NCB flag fluttering aloft on the headstocks. Nothing much had changed in this twilight world beneath the chimneys, among the workshops and boilers and on the spoil heaps that steadily engulfed what remained of the grey abandoned fields.

It was from the flank of one such spoil heap, in my early days of surface surveying, that I saw to my surprise a row of tiny cottages, still inhabited despite the tip's stealthy encroachment, and beside which a tiny tree-fringed pond defied the advancing spoil. As I watched, a laughing, splashing gaggle of young children - boys and girls - stark naked, emerged from the water to continue their frolics in full view on the pond's bank. And although perched there alone with my levelling staff, I turned away in a turmoil of confusion as after making an uninhibited exploration of one another's bodies, one tiny couple embraced and rolled over in the grass to simulate with joyous abandon what they had surely watched adults doing and what to my awakening emotions represented unattainable bliss. I said nothing to Lionel, with whom I was working; what I had been privileged to see seemed too innocent, too beautiful, to deserve a few cheap sniggers.

The surface work I liked most took us away from the sooty buildings and the wheezing, grinding, rattling din of the colliery itself. Tip extensions, proposed railway sidings, new approach roads, subsidence claim surveys - all offered welcome relief from what for me was becoming a pointless, monotonous office routine. Resigned as I was to making no headway in a career for which I was so obviously unsuited, and with what amounted to a junior role that involved the minimum of concentration, I was able to adopt a carefree, almost detached attitude to the work, and to allow my mind to wander unfettered as I held my levelling staff or ranging pole or played out my measuring tape.

Coal had been mined in the locality for centuries. We were on the western edge of the coalfield, which took the form of a basin, and the early miners, working on land leased originally from the abbots of Beauchief Abbey, near Sheffield, began their simple operations in the 14th century. As the coal outcropped along the basin rim, it was easy to obtain and even as late as the 19th century, scores of small mines were still working the shallow seams, operating with primitive horse gins and leaving their abandoned shafts and tiny spoil heaps scattered at random over the honeycombed fields.

Needless to say, these old pits had never been surveyed during their working life. The positions of many were recorded on large-scale Ordnance Survey maps but hitherto unknown shafts were still being discovered, more often than not by chance, the finders sometimes narrowly escaping injury from falling into their hidden depths.

I recalled hearing a story relating to one such lost mine at a rare family gathering, although the giggles and guffaws that greeted it seemed to a child rather excessive. Apparently one of Mother's brothers had been courting a farmer's daughter from a farm near the village but separated from it by an irregular and sloping field known as the Hilly Banks. One night, as the couple were crossing this field after an evening out, the ground beneath their feet gave way and they sank several feet into old mine workings, from which they were eventually rescued after shouting for help. I followed the story with interest up to that point, but the mirth that greeted the comment from one of the men-folk present – that Uncle Ben shouldn't have been pushing so hard – seemed a puzzling and irrelevant observation on an otherwise dramatic tale.

The decision by the NCB to locate, record and fence off these old shafts during that summer meant that our work took us away from the clamour of the modern mines and out into the countryside. We spent long, sunny hours pushing through thorny thickets, tangled briars and nettle clumps in our search for elusive shafts. We hailed farmers on their tractors and intercepted their wives as they crossed cobbled farmyards to feed their hens. On one farm, we ended a lengthy and exasperating interview with a stone-deaf old lady with the discovery that she had mistaken our enquiry about mine shafts for permission to see her garden well.

As with other survey work, my contribution - that of tape-holder and equipment carrier - left me free to soak in the sunshine and the rural calm, to admire passing birds and butterflies, speculate on the history of the farms, fields and woods around us, and ponder what the future held for a misfit whose destiny - comforting though the thought might be - could not be left entirely in the hands of the fates.

But the most enjoyable of these outdoor tasks was yet to come. By happy chance, a triangulation survey covering the entire sub-area was to be carried out before winter set in and the work was commenced soon after the completion of my exams. It involved dividing the area containing the three collieries into huge triangles, similar to the method employed by the Ordnance Survey. Working as a team, we were despatched with our theodolite and ranging poles to measure the heights and distances of the triangles, using a series of hills or expanses of higher ground as vantage points from which to make our observations.

As the complexities of theodolite surveying were considered - and in my case, correctly - beyond the capabilities of trainees, Des, Bert's new assistant David, and myself, were assigned the task of fixing ranging poles at the selected vantage points. We were to remain with them until we received the signal to proceed on our bikes with our poles to the next station. Mr. Elliston, who to begin with took personal charge of the survey, had devised a system of signalling with mirrors, but on overcast days this proved unworkable, and lacking binoculars, we had to rely on a combination of shouts and frantic arm-waving from a link-man cyclist on the nearest road.

To his extreme annoyance, this role was allocated to Lionel. And whereas our duties entailed riding at intervals along country lanes armed with eight-foot ranging poles like latter-day lancers, his time was spent pedalling furiously between the three of us to ensure that we moved our poles as and when required.

It was on one of these errands that Lionel came upon a cosy little wayside inn, that after the triangulation had got under way and Mr. Elliston had relinquished personal control, became our lunchtime rendezvous and unofficial headquarters. Instead of eating our sandwiches alone on our remote hilltops, we were now able to partake of a leisurely and convivial meal, served and presided over by a beaming landlady. Here, I was initiated into the mysterious delights of rough cider, and as a result experienced a loosening of the tongue and unsteadiness of the legs that was to become a source of embarrassment for some time to come.

Pleasant though these occasions were, it was the long and solitary vigils with my ranging pole on the quiet hilltops that redeemed to some extent the disaster of that distant summer. Both Des and David found the inactivity boring; to me however, the enforced idleness was pure balm. I never ceased to marvel that I was being paid the princely sum of six pounds ten shillings a week to sit on a gorse-clad hillside, watching twittering linnets weave their secret ways through the yellow bloom, listening to the constant scraping of the grasshoppers and breathing fresh upland air untainted by the smoke of belching chimneys.

Above all, these soothing summer days afforded me time to think. August, as I well knew, was looming and would bring with it the day of reckoning. Failure in the exams need not necessarily mean the end of my traineeship; re-takes were possible in certain circumstances. But I knew full well that to ask for that concession would be merely to postpone the inevitable, and that I could not bring myself to do. There remained two alternatives: leave the industry and serve my two years in the armed forces, after which I would be free to attempt to embark upon another career; or go into the pit as a linesman when a vacancy occurred, while at the same time studying in the evenings for qualifications in journalism or some other occupation .

But how could I make this choice? Who would advise me? I recalled Bert's words - that there was a world waiting beyond the cramped horizon of the pit tip. Here it lay - or at least, part of it - literally at my feet. And then there was Wilf's reminder that I would need to assert my independence as he had done, and be prepared to toil long hours to get what I wanted. But what *did* I want? To be a writer, yes, but was the world of newspaper journalism really what I was destined for? I was unsure of that, even. The only writing I had done since leaving school over a year before had been confined to a diary, thank-you letters at Christmas, and a handful of faltering little poems. Even my cricket sketches, for which I had been admonished at school, were things of the past, doomed, it seemed, like my short cricketing career, to oblivion.

One thing was certain. Two men, different as chalk and cheese, would need to know of my intentions fairly soon. Mr. Elliston, I knew, would hear me out patiently and sympathetically, perhaps even proffer some badly needed advice. The other's reaction I could only guess at, but I feared the worst - Father.

Rather than raise the matter in front of Mother, I decided to drop my bombshell in the workshop. She would be put in the picture soon enough but to begin with I hoped that, without the need to placate Mother, Father might just listen to my reasoning, weigh up the pros and cons and offer his judgement without flying into one of his violent tempers.

Shirtsleeves rolled above his elbows, his ever-present pencil jutting from behind his ear beneath the cloth cap, he was bent in concentration over the bench as I entered.

'Now my lad, how've you got on?' It was his usual greeting, delivered without looking up. He was sixty-seven - beyond the age at which most men I knew, certainly miners, had retired. They sat on their haunches by the miners' welfare wall, toothless, gaunt - finished. I'd only discovered Father's age by furtive enquiry; even Mother professed to be uncertain at first. He would never retire; he'd work until he dropped. The alternative was idleness and that, in his book, was worse than death itself.

My mouth went dry. I had to force the words out and they broke the silence with a rush, harsh and awkward. I said I knew I'd failed the exams. I could either do my national service and then attempt a new career, such as journalism, or be demoted to linesman and study at home or at evening class and leave the pit later. I stopped, breathless, fearful of saying too much, going too far. But Father had not followed beyond my first sentence.

'Fail? What do you mean, fail?' he thundered incredulously. 'Never heard such piffle! How do you know you've failed?' My heart sank. How could I possibly make him understand - a man who refused to recognise failure even if it stared him in the face. I tried again. I attempted to explain that not only was I convinced that I would never make a surveyor but that I didn't want to be one. I'd rather do my national service or go down the pit - anything rather than go on as now. This was more than Father could bear. Blind rage was his only weapon when uncomfortable truths threatened.

'Then bogger off down the bloddy pit!' he bellowed, flinging down the plane he had been using, '- and bogger off out of here as well!'

Tears choking, I took him at his word and made for the door.

'But I'll tell you this,' he shouted as I shut it behind me. 'You'll not go in the army - or if you do, you'll never darken our door again!'

# Chapter 13

**F**our doors below our 1920s semi stood a large detached house, the last to be built alongside the road leading from the village past the lane to the colliery and on to the nearest town. Standing in spacious grounds and set well back from the road, it had been built just before the war by a retired factory owner from the town, who had died soon afterwards, leaving his childless widow alone in their vast, newly-erected residence.

Father, who had some time before bought a strip of land extending behind the other semis and up to what had become the boundary of the new house, was soon on affable terms with the newcomers - a friendship of sorts which continued, in the form of lengthy over-the-fence chats, with the widow.

Mrs Fairbrother was a small, active woman. She had once been a schoolteacher and her somewhat brusque manner and dogmatic tone of voice didn't exactly endear her to Mother, who referred to her as Lady Muck and branded her - to Father and me at least - as 'Mutton dressed as lamb.' At our first meeting, I had been surprised at how much she knew about me. This came about, I learned later, through her friendship with another retired teacher, whose pupil I had once been at the village school and who had, unknown to me, formed a favourable impression of my ability at composition.

Mrs Fairbrother's surprise at my leaving school without matriculating was as nothing compared with her astonishment at my entering the mining industry. Meeting her in the street, I braced myself for the searching questions that I knew would follow - questions on the progress of my studies and prospects of promotion - which I answered falteringly and unhappily under the scrutiny of her penetrating gaze. Since I started work, she had developed the habit of lending me books - via Father over the fence - on a range of subjects, including history, travel and literature. Father usually passed them on without comment, but Mother was quick to point out that we were quite capable of buying our own books and didn't need 'Lady Muck, showing off what she's got.'

In the uneasy calm that followed the scene in the workshop, Father broke the silence one evening as we ate.

'Mrs Fairbrother wants you to go round and choose your own books. She says she can't remember what you've had.' Mother gave her customary 'Tch, tch' of annoyance. I promised to go round that evening.

On my infrequent previous visits I had never ventured beyond the sumptuously furnished living room. This evening, however, Mrs Fairbrother showed me into another spacious room she called the study. Bewildered, I found myself surrounded by shelf upon shelf of books - books on every conceivable subject, all arranged in immaculate order, some, with leather-bound spines, beyond my reach on the uppermost shelves. What few gaps remained round the walls were occupied by paintings, framed maps and sepia photographs of the late Mr. Fairbrother, standing by a long-bonneted car and overlooking dramatic views. I made my choice and returned to the living room. Mrs. Fairbrother commanded me to sit opposite her and subjected me to another of her searching questioning sessions, this time on my reasons for selecting the books. That done, seemingly to her satisfaction, she turned to other matters.

'Your father tells me that you are giving up your surveying studies,' she began. 'I must say' - one of her favourite expressions -'that I'm not in the least surprised.' I started in my chair. 'It struck me as an odd choice - most odd.' I wondered what was coming next. 'He also tells me that you want to do your national service but that for some strange reason he is set against it.' By now I was on the edge of my seat, straining to anticipate what else lay in store. I hadn't long to wait. 'I get the impression that your parents are fearful that you will be contaminated by army life.' She gave a dry chuckle. '- though how they can possibly believe that working down the pit is somehow less of a hazard in that sense I can't begin to understand.'

She now came to what was clearly the object of my visit. 'Anyway, I understand that to avoid national service you will need to remain in mining until you are twenty-six. That may sound a very long time.' How right she was! It sounded like an age. The despair I felt must have been all too evident. She went on:

'But if you take my advice, you'll make a start preparing for your future straight away.' I made a faltering attempt to assure her that I'd every intention of doing so. Mrs. Fairbrother, however, was into her stride by now and had no intention of being interrupted. 'I've told your father that you should be using your strengths, which I understand, lie in English and history. He said something to the effect that you had expressed an interest in journalism. Tell me about it.'

Seizing the opportunity, I launched into a detailed account of my writing attainments, which, I realised with dismay, sounded dreadfully meagre. Then, tentatively, I mentioned having written some poetry.

'Bring it round for me to see,' came the command. I promised to comply the following day.

\*\*\*\*\*\*\*\*\*\*\*\*\*\*\*\*

Somewhat sheepishly, Father handed me the envelope containing the poems.

'Mrs. Fairbrother gave me these – said she liked 'em'. He cleared his throat. 'Didn't know you'd written anything –

99

like this'. I wondered if he'd read them and if so, what his reaction had been.

'Anyroad up,' he went on, the old conviction back in his voice now that the awkward preliminaries were safely over. 'She's given me this – out of her paper. All about studying at home. We'll send off for it and see what they say – can't do any harm'.

He proffered the cutting. 'Study at home with the Bennett College', I read. Then the slogan at the foot of the advertisement caught my eye. 'Let me be your Father.' If Father had noticed it, he didn't let on.

Father was highly impressed by the prospectus. It was a most comprehensive affair, offering courses in every subject we could think of – and a lot more besides. The cover photograph of the college itself was imposing too; it was in Sheffield, a city Father knew well, having helped to repair bomb damage there immediately after the war. Eventually he found the section he was looking for.

'Here we are,' he said triumphantly, '-journalism!' He read the course outline out aloud in the way he read items that took his fancy from the *Daily Express*. There was no mistaking his verdict as he came to the end.

'Sounds all right to me. You can tell they know what they're talking about.' He turned to the notes at the beginning and putting on his reading-aloud voice once more, read us the extract about inviting the college's representative to visit to provide full details concerning specific courses. 'Right-o,' he announced, 'we'll fill this in and get him to call. Pass me that pen and ink, Mother.'

The evening of the arranged visit soon arrived. We had tea earlier than usual and while Mother went upstairs to change her frock, Father stripped to the waist at the kitchen sink and after securing his razor strop to the tap, sharpened his cut-throat and had one of his rare evening shaves before donning his best trousers and a clean shirt. I was somewhat taken aback when he insisted on having the envelope of poems handy but hastened to comply.

As instructed, I answered the awaited knock and showed the elderly red-faced visitor, dressed in a navy blue suit and carrying an important-looking briefcase, into the living room, where Mother and Father, looking - to my eyes at least - as though they were trying hard to appear casual, were waiting.

If the representative was expecting to have to pull out all the stops to gain a new student, he was in for a pleasant surprise. On the contrary, Father's line of approach was to enquire whether I would be suitable for the course, and to make a case for my acceptance, the climax of which was to produce my poems and to invite the man to read them. This he somewhat uncomfortably began to do, watched closely by Father, who after the man had made a few appreciative grunts, demanded to know what he thought of them. He was, he said, very impressed. Father beamed.

Eventually, the man raised the subject of payment, and began to outline the various ways in which this could be made. Father, however, was ready. Banknotes to cover the entire fee were at hand. The deal was done and Mother was despatched to make a celebratory pot of tea. Next day, I broke the news to Mrs. Fairbrother. Her face creased even more into a knowing smile.

'I  knew he'd see sense in the end,' she said, 'I must say, his bark's worse than his bite. Now just you see that you make a go of it this time. Remember - it's what you wanted to do.' I thanked her. 'Let me know how you get on,' she commanded. 'And remember too, my books are here whenever you need them.'

There remained Mr Elliston. Buoyed up by my relief over the course, I found breaking the news easier than I had feared. Even so, I had to be certain that a place could be found for me as a linesman; I knew that under the new policy each colliery was to have two linesmen but I couldn't assume that an opening would be there for the asking.

Mr. Elliston made no attempt to conceal his disappointment. He had, he said, been well satisfied with the standard of my work. However, he realised that I had not made my decision lightly and was sure that a vacancy on the linesman staff would arise in the not- too- distant future. Like Mrs. Fairbrother, he raised the question of national service; was I certain that I was embarking on the right course of action? I was far from certain but I chose to sidestep the question; it had been Father's decision, not mine, and I could well imagine Alf's contemptuous reaction at what he would see as my abject capitulation. But I was a woefully naive seventeen-year-old who, despite a year at work, was still inadequately prepared for the independence that many of my contemporaries took for granted.

***************

The results were much as I had feared. Only my geology was - to my mind at least - remotely satisfactory; the rest reflected my utter unsuitability for mine surveying. By agreement with Mr Elliston, I let it be known that I would not be continuing with my studies but that I would remain on the staff pending a vacancy arising for a linesman. As the ambition of most poorly-paid linesmen was to obtain appointments as trainee surveyors, my move - in the opposite direction - was greeted with something approaching incredulity, which the passing mention that I intended embarking on studies of a different nature did little to dispel. Lionel, in particular, voiced his bewilderment.

'Once you're down the pit, it's a hell of a job getting out,' he declared, adding the sombre warning that I was to be given countless times in the coming years: 'Once a miner, always a miner.'

Alf, who I had feared would openly ridicule my decision, was more circumspect. I learned that one of his relatives was a journalist on a regional paper and his prospects were good. 'No scrabbling around a bloody pit for him,' he said pointedly. 'If you can knuckle down and slog as he has, you'll end up laughing at poor sods like us.'

With my boats now well and truly burnt, it was up to me to prove Alf right and Lionel wrong.

# Chapter 14

Ten years had passed since my first and only acquaintance with the sea. As a seven-year-old, a week at Skegness had been a never-to-be-forgotten experience, with not just sand, but shows, charabancs and exotic gardens. Now, a decade later, and one of an exuberant crowd of club members and their leaders, I was bound for the coast once again - this time to sample the delights of a holiday camp on the outskirts of Morecambe.

I doubt whether I could have been more impressed by a tropical island. For a whole week I was suddenly and miraculously free - not just from the uncertainties of the future but also from the restraints of home life. And I was among friends; youths of my own age, girls too; everyone on a trembling peak of anticipation - of what, I suspect we knew not, but that didn't concern us; we were out to enjoy ourselves and the non-stop hedonistic novelty of it all held us in thrall.

Of Morecambe itself - derided by Mother as being in Blackpool's shadow - we saw but little. We had no need of its extra allure; everything we could hope for was there, on site, for our instant gratification and we immersed ourselves in it all like lambs in clover.

As an only child, conceived - if Mother's occasional bitter outbursts were indeed true - by accident, I had witnessed the family life of other boys with a mixture of envy and bewilderment. Yet now, I found myself safely embedded in the midst of a carefree band of brothers and sisters; the phrase 'One big happy family' not only acquired a meaning but became, for me, a warm, enveloping reality. And the notion of family didn't end there. For our club leader and his jolly wife, together with a little band of other adults - who Mother would have labelled disparagingly as 'Chapel folk' -

let it be known from the outset that this was their holiday too, and they were determined to enjoy it for all they were worth.

And so we paddled, swam, played beach cricket and rounders, sampled every form of amusement on offer and mingled easily and happily with other campers. Des and Jose, together with Joan and Paul, the youth who had taken over as her escort following my inadequate dithering, seldom joined in our activities and sly winks and dark hints were passed round as to what alternative pastimes they were indulging in. Overhearing one such whispered suggestion, I became the object of much teasing after enquiring in all innocence: 'What is it, exactly, that Des is hoping to get his leg over?'

The beach cricket, in particular, delighted me. After my demoralising failure to break into the serious competitive game, here was the chance to play for the sheer love of it. I swung my bat with abandon, toppled wickets with ease and plucked soft-ball catches effortlessly out of the air. Seeking a sterner test, we let it be known that we welcomed matches with other groups and managed to defeat both teams that responded to the challenge. In amongst both runs and wickets, I was heady with success; surely there could be no other sensation left to add to this feast of delights?

\*\*\*\*\*\*\*\*\*\*\*\*\*\*\*\*\*

But there was. In our evening wanderings around the camp, our group made contact with a similar sized party of factory girls from Bradford. Time was precious; we had to work fast. In one hectic afternoon on the following day, we managed to pair off and to my amazement I found myself alone with a smiling, dark-haired girl in a flowery white frock, who returned wet, eager kisses and greeted my every trite remark with laughing appreciation. Arms locked, we wandered aimlessly through wonderland, pausing only to exchange more kisses, oblivious of the rest of humanity, relegating it to a mere backdrop role for our bliss. Mercilessly, time sped by and our week was over. Farewell kisses were snatched, solemn promises to write made, emotional waves exchanged through glinting coach windows and we were on our way. For me at least, it had been more than a holiday - it had been a long-overdue awakening.

******************

Back at work, Mr Elliston had news for me. The linesman at Hallfield Colliery, in the next sub-area, would be leaving in September and I would be taking his place. To enable me to get to know the ropes, he had arranged for me to begin work there in a fortnight's time. As Walter Thorne, the Hallfield surveyor, was based at area headquarters, I would in future be responsible to him but he hoped that I would keep in touch. In any case, he had come across something that he thought might be of future use to me and he suggested that I call at his home on one evening in the following week. Grateful, though mystified, I resumed my work.

Although Alf had reacted calmly enough to the news of my forthcoming departure, our relationship deteriorated markedly as we worked our last shifts underground together. I had got into the habit of exchanging a few words of banter with some of the men we passed on our travels and after one such brief halt, Alf snapped at me irritably, accusing me of time-wasting and of being over- familiar with men who, he clearly implied, were our inferiors.

I smouldered at the injustice of these remarks and followed by Colin, strode off briskly towards our working place, assuming that Alf was following on behind. Eventually, with no sign of his lamp, we sat down at a junction to wait. Time passed, and with still no distant lamp visible, I asked Colin to wait while I retraced my steps to the spot where we had left Alf. Finding no sign, I went further back - to the junction at which I had talked to the workmen. One of them thought he had seen Alf take the other - and much longer route - to the district where we were working. Relieved, yet annoyed and puzzled, I returned to Colin and we continued along the direct route to our workplace.

Alf was waiting for us. Deaf to our insistence that we had arrived by the usual route, he called us - and me in particular - every obscenity in his extensive and colourful vocabulary. We let this torrent of abuse flow over our heads, knowing Alf's anger would eventually burn itself out. It was only later that it dawned on me exactly why he had over-reacted so alarmingly. The junction at which Colin and I had waited in vain was the place at which the fatal roof fall had occurred a few weeks earlier. Alf couldn't bring himself to confess his fear to a couple of juniors and had instead trudged off alone on a lengthy detour to avoid the dreaded place.

Despite the strain that now existed in my relationship with Alf, I found myself experiencing a pang of regret at leaving Birch Park. It was a small, friendly pit and, amazing though it later seemed, I had come to regard its ramshackle, outdated surface features and cramped underground workings with something approaching affection. I would miss too, the walk across the fields and the chats I had once had with Alf. Thankfully however, our parting turned out to be not only civil but friendly. The old warm twinkle and slowly-spreading grin returned as we took our leave. After half-conceding that his behaviour had been rather difficult of late, he wished me well for the future.

'Remember - it's not the pit work that matters - that's just a means to an end,' he said. 'Put everything you've got into your course - and I'll be watching out for your name in the headlines.'

Des, of course, I would be seeing at the youth club. Bert and Lionel - whose teasing since Morecambe I had inwardly relished - gave me a bawdy send-off on my final afternoon in the office; Des, it seemed, had allowed his vivid imagination full play in describing my holiday exploits. As I mounted my bike at the day's end, Lionel bestowed a parting accolade:

'You can see it's not the first time he's got his leg over!' He was wrong. The next time would be the first. But at least I knew now what he meant.

***************

Mr and Mrs Elliston welcomed me into their home like an honoured guest. To my surprise, they lived in a modest semi, far older than my own, on a mean street not far from the chapel at which the youth club was based. They broke off from the *Manchester Guardian* crossword and we talked on a range of topics before my host produced his gift - his cricket flannels and sweater, which he was sure I would put to good use in the coming season. Gratefully, I thanked him and cycled homeward, warmed by his insistence that I visit again. My mind turned to cricket. Yes, perhaps I could yet resurrect my hitherto lacklustre career - if time allowed in what promised to be a busy life ahead.

# Chapter 15

Hallfield Colliery was about four miles north of my home, on the edge both of the coalfield and of the village after which it was named, which straddled the main road to Chesterfield. It was a small mine, about the size of Birch Park, and like it, had a long history. That history was a colourful one; in 1875, it leapt into national prominence when it was bought outright by the Derbyshire and Yorkshire miners' union, who operated it for some time until the men went on strike following the introduction of economy measures intended to reduce working costs.

A few lingering traces of this independent, go-it-alone attitude still persisted, reinforced no doubt by its remote location. It was in every sense a rural pit, set in open countryside surrounded by fields and woods and worked to a large degree by men who maintained an active interest in the land, and who regarded mining coal as a means of supplementing a livelihood as smallholders. Like Oakwood Manor, Hallfield had originally been a shaft mine but by nationalisation, much of the coal was mined from an adit, driven into rising ground on the flank of a slope above a shallow valley. As with most adits, conditions were often wet and men working in the dampest places sometimes wore gumboots, which reinforced the rural impression.

Fortunately for me, the colliery was close to a bus route. The only disadvantage immediately apparent was that there were no pithead baths, which meant that I would have to travel to and from work in my pit clothes. Mother, predictably, was appalled. Including my working clothes in her Monday morning wash was bad enough; the prospect of her son walking up the road from the bus stop in his grime for all to see was one of personal humiliation. Whatever would the neighbours think?

To my surprise, I learned that I wouldn't lose touch entirely with office work. Unlike the colliery-based linesmen in Mr Elliston's sub-area, who worked underground full-time, my appointment was as a staff linesman and as such, I would report to area office on Saturday mornings to receive my instructions from my immediate superior, Walter Thorne. And so, on the Saturday before commencing at Hallfield, I renewed acquaintance with the dingy, two-storey office block at which I had been appointed as a trainee some sixteen months earlier. This time however, instead of being ushered into the Area Chief's domain, I found myself joining what seemed a milling throng in the main survey office, where a quietly spoken, somewhat diffident man in his late thirties introduced himself as Walter Thorne and then called over Ken, the linesman I was to succeed.

I spent what proved to be a profitable and reassuring morning, studying plans of the Hallfield workings so that I would be able to find my way around when the time came. I would have the following week with Ken, after which I would be expected to work independently, assisted by a youth straight from school, who would be based at the colliery. My questions answered and my doubts - most of them, at least - put to rest, I joined the exodus clattering down the stairs and out into the street. So far so good; the real test would come in the following week.

Although I had travelled by bus to Oakwood Manor in my pit clothes with Lionel and Des, the Monday morning walk down to the bus stop was an odd experience. There were no other miners on the bus, or at least none dressed for work as I was; Hallfield was the only remaining pit for several miles around without baths and to my knowledge no-one in the village worked there. I settled into my top-deck seat apparently unnoticed; the other passengers, chiefly office and shop workers, carried on with their chatting or continued burrowing into their newspapers. I enjoyed the ride, with its sweeping views westwards towards the lower slopes of the Peak District - countryside I was just beginning to get to know intimately on my weekend bike rides and which, with its villages of stone-built cottages set higgledy-piggledy along twisting narrow streets, held a growing appeal.

Not that Hallfield belonged to the Peakland scene; sadly, its coal reserves had seen to that. It had a scatter of mellow gritstone houses and one or two good looking farms, but a red-brick rash had spread across its once fair face and its proud and ancient church tower presided over a hotch-potch of streets of dwellings of every conceivable style and material.

I had arranged to meet Ken in the lamp-room, one of a cluster of buildings huddled together at the foot of a winding lane off the main road through the village. Compared with the other pits I knew, Birch Park included, everything about Hallfield Colliery appeared to be reduced in scale as I approached that September morning. Even the chimney and the spoil heap looked strangely tiny, as though reluctant to mar the backdrop of hedged fields stretching away into the far distance, while the two sets of squat headstocks resembled a working model rather than the real thing.

The lamp room, I soon discovered, was not simply a convenient meeting place. It was in turn a newsroom, a debating chamber, a theatre, and on occasion, a sanctuary, to which all manner of men were drawn, and in which everyone was given a warm and - in my case, at least - effusive welcome. Ken, who had recently gained his deputy's certificate, and was commencing his coal-face experience the following week, carried out introductions in a way that would have done Mr Elliston proud. My first handshake exchange was with Ezra, the senior lamp-room attendant, followed by Bill, his assistant, and as I was soon to discover, his loyal lieutenant. Then, as though from nowhere, appeared several others, whose roles I failed to establish at the time, but who later emerged as characters in their own right in the day-to-day life of this unique little colliery.

Introductions over, Ken went on to explain that the lamp-room was in fact my base. I was shown a cupboard in which my equipment was kept safely under lock and key; there was room inside too for any personal belongings, such as spare clothing, that I might wish to leave. On days when my work took me down the adit, Ken advised, I would find it best to leave my snap in my cupboard until the end of the shift. Seeing my puzzled expression, he reminded me that conditions below were extremely wet, and that I was free to walk out of the adit as soon as I had finished work. I could then eat my sandwiches in the lamp-room while my outer clothes were put to dry out - another service offered by the friendly lamp men.

I spent the week accompanying Ken on a comprehensive tour of the workings. This entailed descending the main winding shaft to reach the older, deeper parts of the mine, as well as walking down the adit to visit the more recent workings. I had encountered wet conditions down the Oakwood Manor adit but they were as nothing compared with those that confronted me now. In places the water poured from fissures in the roof like a never-ending cloudburst - foul-smelling water, varying in colour from dark brown to clayey yellow. This relentless downpour led to numerous roof falls and a continuous battle was being waged to prevent a major inundation; pumps throbbed non-stop and roof supports were being constantly renewed.

Considering the appalling conditions in which they had to work, the men - 'watter rats' to their fellow miners - were amazingly cheerful and good-humoured. True, they were paid a special bonus in recognition of the privations they faced daily, but to the uninitiated such as me, no extra payment, however large, could possibly compensate for the danger and discomfort their work entailed.

During our tour of the dry deep workings, I had noticed evidence of mice - chewed snap bags - and knowing that these creatures usually arrived below ground in sacks of pony fodder, I asked a deputy if they managed to survive down the adit, where ponies were also employed.

'Oh aye - the crafty little buggers have grown webbed feet,' came the reply. Having enjoyed his jest, he said that although he had not encountered mice in the wet conditions, rats were occasionally seen, lured down the adit by scraps of leftover food.

We spent the Friday afternoon touring the surface installations. Wherever we went, we were greeted with ready grins and good-natured banter, Ken receiving good wishes for the next stage in his career and I being welcomed to 'our pit' as though into a family firm.

\*\*\*\*\*\*\*\*\*\*\*\*\*\*\*\*\*

As the bus drew near my stop and I clanked down the stairs in my heavy boots, I could see Mrs Fairbrother, standing with her shopping on the boarding platform. We alighted and I took the heavier of her bags. As we climbed the hill she referred in passing to my new job but appeared not to notice my blackened face and working clothes. What really concerned her was my correspondence course, which to her obvious satisfaction I was about to commence. As we parted, I smiled to myself at the thought of Mother's face if she could have seen me walking in my pit dirt alongside one of the wealthiest and best-dressed women in the village. The shame of it! But then, perhaps the sight was not as incongruous as all that - after all, Mother often referred to her as Lady Muck.

# Chapter 16

My life now took on what proved to be a satisfying pattern. After returning home and washing off the bulk of my dirt before the kitchen fire in the manner of the colliers of old, I completed my ablutions in the bathroom upstairs, dressed, and settled down to read my *Manchester Guardian*. To Mr. Elliston's satisfaction, I had decided to place a regular order for the paper before leaving Swainsbrook and soon realised that Neville Cardus's cricket articles were merely a small part of the mental stimulation it offered.

Except on Fridays - youth club night - my evenings were devoted to my correspondence course. It required only a cursory glance at the first lesson to realise that there was a world of difference between writing a reasonably good school essay and producing saleable work. Even so, my tutor's comments on my first attempts were sufficiently encouraging to spur me on, while the lessons themselves sharpened my powers of observation and prompted me not merely to widen my reading but to do so with a more critical eye.

My pit work was made all the more congenial by my relationship with my new workmates. Derek, my assistant linesman, a fresh-faced country lad straight from school, was quiet and even-tempered; his life revolved around his father's smallholding and in exchange for an occasional enquiry on the well-being of the family's livestock, I received in return his wholehearted co-operation. But it was in Walter Thorne, the unit surveyor and my immediate superior, that I was most fortunate. On one of our first shifts together underground, he had mentioned his love of classical music, and the pleasure he derived from listening to the afternoon symphony concert on the wireless as he washed, following a shift down the pit.

There and then I resolved to follow his example. That afternoon, a new source of pleasure entered my life. It so happened that after a short overture, the orchestra went on to perform Mozart's Eine Kleine Nachtmusik. I was enchanted. Until that day, my musical appreciation had been confined to snatches of popular classics, endured with mounting impatience by Father, who branded anything more profound than Gershwin as 'heavy', or by Mother, who would invariable suggest that the musicians were 'making it up as they went along.' Now, however, I had the kitchen to myself, and could listen uninterrupted as I washed, all the while adding new discoveries to my repertoire.

One afternoon, on arriving home and opening the kitchen door, I could hear the murmur of unfamiliar voices coming from the living room. Visitors of any kind were rare, and were confined more or less to a handful of Mother's friends and relations, most of whom called in the evening. I was in something of a dilemma. Visitors usually entered and left by the kitchen door; only in exceptional circumstances was the locked-and-bolted front door opened. My towel and flannel were in their accustomed place by the sink; dare I risk stripping and washing off my dirt? What if the door should suddenly open and the unknown visitors enter? I thought of tapping on the living room door and announcing my arrival but knowing Mother's discomfort at my appearance, my old diffidence returned and I hesitated, unsure of what to do.

At last, I decided to take the risk and start my wash. Reluctantly depriving myself of my orchestral concert, so that I could detect any movement next door, I cautiously began to peel off the dirty clothes, while in the meantime running my hot water. Once I had washed off most of the dirt, I could wrap myself in my towel and make a dash for the stairs and the safety of the bathroom. But my calculations were thrown into disarray when the inner door was flung open. I had barely time to grab my towel before staring inquisitively at me on firmly planted feet was a little girl with ribboned plaits, followed closely by her grandmother, a cousin of Mother's, who although living quite near, was a very infrequent visitor.

Mother hastened to explain the unusual circumstances; Aunt Agnes, however, jolly as ever, paid little heed. My towel by now safely in place, I was given one of the enthusiastic kisses I recalled with pleasure from childhood encounters. This was followed by an equally enthusiastic, if somewhat wetter kiss from her vivacious granddaughter, who on being told that she had picked up a black smudge on her face in the process, demanded to see herself in a mirror, and was clearly pleased with the result.

*****************

Despite the appalling conditions, I enjoyed my work. Extending the whitewashed lines in the wetter parts of the adit workings was a near impossibility, but the men were used to checking their own alignment using oil lamps suspended from screw hooks and all I had to do was to fix new hooks as the workings advanced. By contrast, the shaft workings were virtually dry, although traces of dampness along some of the roadways provided ideal conditions for certain kinds of fungus. One, which was almost pure white and resembled candyfloss, hung in great festoons from the wooden roof supports and in places took on a ghostly effect when revealed by the beams of our lamps. Other, smaller growths proved on examination to be clusters of tiny toadstools, varying in colour from grey to yellow, and sometimes speckled with microscopic insects.

Mice, too, thrived in these deeper workings. Their ancestors must have been brought down the mine in sacks of pony fodder and true to their reputation, they bred prolifically and had colonised extensive areas of the workings, living in the pack - the walls of the roadways built from blasted rock. As both men and ponies ate their snap in these roadways, which were constantly extended, so the mice followed, finding ample sustenance in the leftovers and even venturing out boldly from their crevices while the men were eating. Because of the heat, face workers left their coats, together with their snap bags, hanging in the roadway, a short distance from their workplace. No-one would dream of leaving anything remotely edible in his coat pocket however; the universal snap tin was the only way of ensuring that the sandwiches remained intact. Occasionally the youthful pony gangers would amuse themselves at snap time by putting a few crumbs inside a tilted glass bottle and switching off their lamps. The silence that followed would soon be broken by the excited squeaks of the mice as they scrambled in search of the food. When this was located, lamps were switched on and the unfortunate rodents were bombarded with lumps of rock in their glass prison.

Seldom if ever were the ponies subjected to cruelty. On the contrary, a strong bond of affection was often built up between the ganger and his pony. The dozen or so ponies were housed in clean and ventilated stables near the pit bottom, under the watchful eye of a veteran miner well versed in their welfare. The 'wretched blind pit ponies', whose plight moved the poet to anger half a century before, had long since disappeared and although they were still called upon to draw heavy loads of timber along low roadways, these ponies were well fed and cared for. Unlike their fellows employed down the shaft mine, which saw the light of day only during the pit's summer holiday, the adit ponies came to the surface at the end of the shift and were stabled in a small field on the edge of the colliery. The wet conditions in which they worked necessitated a thorough cleaning-down before they were left to enjoy their fodder and fresh bedding.

Many were the stories told about pit ponies. It was often said that they could find their way throughout the part of the mine in which they worked without any light to guide them; certainly, they coped amazingly well with only their ganger's lamp providing illumination. It was generally agreed that they possessed some way of gauging the passing of time, and would become agitated, uncooperative even, if pressed to continue working beyond their normal hours. It was noticeable too, that when on their way back towards the stables at the end of the shift, they would quicken their pace as they approached their destination.

Some miners believed that ponies also had the ability to detect danger. Examples were cited of their strange behaviour immediately before a roof fall; this is perhaps not as surprising as it may at first seem, for a large fall often began with a trickle of small particles, and a pony struck by these was more than likely to react by showing distress, even by bolting.

Derek, my assistant, had a winning way with ponies. He seemed to carry an inexhaustible supply of crusts, apples, and other delicacies around with him and whenever we descended the shaft we would make a point of taking a short diversion through the stables so that he could offer these titbits to Tich, a small ageing pony of which he was especially fond. Although Tich's stall was some distance from the stables entrance, the little pony never failed to give a whinny of anticipation at our approach. After a long working life, Tich now carried out light duties on the night shift and we knew that he would soon be pensioned off, to spend his final days out to grass, thanks to a sympathetic purchaser - unlike generations of his kind that ended up in the knacker's yard.

Survey team, Swainsbrook, 1950s. Author fourth from left

Youth club holiday, Morecambe. Author fourth from left, back row.

Birch Park. A small friendly pit.

Hallfield. A country coalmine.

Stage debut. A poised, polished man-of-the-world?

The old windmill. 'A place of pilgrimage.'

Thorpe Cloud, Dovedale. 'A reward beyond price.'

Eyam. A poignant reminder of the plague.

Leicestershire. Every church faithfully photographed.

Rutland. Meeting one of the locals.

## *The Worst Batsman?*

In cricket, as in many other sports, the unpredictable frequently happens. Cricket lovers scrutinising the score sheet on Thursday morning, however, must have mistrusted either the printer's accuracy or their own eyesight when the figure 47 appeared opposite the name of Hollies in the Warwickshire first innings against Sussex. This was no mistake, however; the veteran spin bowler had in fact surpassed his previous highest score – 24 runs against Leicestershire in 1937. Does this mean that the unofficial honour of being the worst batsman in first-class cricket is vacant, assuming that the title belonged to Hollies (who is no doubt highly amused about the whole affair)? Each of the counties, no doubt, can offer a player worthy of this unique position, for the feat of taking 100 wickets in a season before scoring 100 runs has been frequently achieved.

The legendary Tom Emmett, who bowled for Yorkshire for many a year, was said to have been one of the worst batsmen who ever strode to the crease and the story that the groundsman's horse at a certain ground used to back itself into the roller shafts when Emmett emerged from the pavilion is still told with relish by long-memoried Yorkists.

Published - and paid (14/6d) - by 'The Manchester Guardian.'

Village children, Derbyshire. A happy - and significant - encounter.

Cotswold perfection. Chipping Campden.

The Rollright Stones. Strange and sinister.

A welcome break from studying.

The Quantocks, Somerset. Honeymoon country.

# Chapter 17

My love of the countryside, which had lain virtually dormant since boyhood, awoke with a compelling urgency in the spring of 1949. I had found joy and wonderment then in the fields and woods close to home, oblivious of the pits and the relentless encroachment of ugliness. Now, I wanted to see for myself the open upland country of the Peak District, as depicted in alluring sepia photographs in my growing library. Here awaiting me were sweeping views, rugged rocky outcrops, romantic ruined castles and great houses rich in historic associations. Above all, I wanted to explore every facet of this other, wilder Derbyshire and in so doing, get to know it as deeply and intimately as a close and valued friend.

To begin with, I had to have a bike. My sit-up-and-beg Hercules - held in contempt ever since the day, two years earlier, when Bert had gently teased me in front of Enid - had served its purpose. It had carried me on my first weekend journeys of discovery into the foothills of the Peak, but its limitations could no longer be ignored. I was told of a sports bike for sale in the next village, paid the fourteen pounds asking price demanded, and rode home in triumph like a conquering hero. My savings had gone but I now had the means to realise my ambition, or at least part of it.

That spring, as the evenings, rich in promise, lengthened, I rode out into the nearest stretch of open countryside after my wash and returned home ravenously hungry and radiantly happy. Evening meal over, I turned my attention to my course, seeking whenever possible to write on some aspect of the countryside. As well as the *Manchester Guardian*, I was now subscribing to the *Derbyshire Countryside* magazine, and the height of my ambition was to see an article under my name included within its glossy pages.

Friday evenings remained the highlight of the week. Weather permitting, the youth club met on the nearby recreation ground for rounders and it was with quiet satisfaction that I leaned my sporty-looking bike against the chapel wall alongside those of other members before joining in the fun. The weekend atmosphere added an extra glow to the proceedings; for although there was still the following morning's session in the survey office, this was no hardship, for the afternoon was free and the whole of Sunday was mine to discover more Peak District delights.

Meanwhile, the rounders games provided the ideal means of strengthening bonds with other youths and to extending my limited experience with girls. There was plenty of laughter, excitement, dropped catches, fumbling attempts at running-out and the exhilarating thrill at being cheered in on completing a rounder. And the girls, with their white blouses and flowing skirts - girls I had seen often enough in the crowded clubroom on winter evenings - suddenly became radiant, slender, desirable beings, amazingly accessible, yet infinitely mysterious still to one whose experience had hitherto been confined to a few fleeting days at Morecambe.

One girl in particular - fair, quick moving, slightly-built - stood out from the rest. We had exchanged a few pleasantries during indoor meetings and a certain quiet intensity about her had impressed me. I learned that she was a devout chapel member and Sunday school teacher and that her father was a miner who had been a capable cricketer in his day. To my surprise, my interest in this girl had been noticed by at least one member of the group to which I had become attached.

'Tha'll get nowt from Rita Kitts, tha' knows,' he remarked casually. 'Tha'll be lucky if o'll even guh out wi' thee - let alone let thee touch 'er.' I winced. Mentally, I had already put Rita on a pedestal, from which she would in time descend, graciously agreeing to accompany me on weekend bike rides into the Peak. If touching her meant what my informant's leer implied, it hadn't even entered my head, but I could hardly tell him that.

'Anyroad, they reckon o' fancies Ron Dobson,' the youth went on. '- allus 'angin' abaht when 'e's around. Dunna think much o' thy chances there.'

Ron, suave and aloof, was also a chapel member, several years older than the rest of us and an accomplished pianist, attending the club only infrequently. I was taken aback by what I heard but did my best to hide it. The pedestal was still in place and as there was no other likely contender in view, I resolved to try my luck.

What I at first took for a flush of pleasure turned out to be one of embarrassment. It wasn't that she was unwilling to go out with me, Rita explained at some length. It was just that the weekends were so busy, what with shopping on Saturdays and chapel on Sundays. I fell back on my second line of approach - a short evening bike ride. Again, the response was discouraging. Every evening of the week, it seemed, was spoken for; rituals, religious and domestic, lay claim to every hour of Rita's time away from her hosiery factory bench. She stressed how sorry she was to have to turn down my offer and seemed sincere. Was her supposed devotion to Dobson responsible for my rejection, I wondered? The disappointment was keen but not exactly demoralising. I decided to put the pedestal to one side for the time being and extend my search; surely somewhere there was a pretty girl with carefree ways, time to spare, and with her feet planted firmly on the ground - which was where I intended them to remain.

Barbara seemed such a girl. Tall and dark, with a ready smile and a crackly, infectious laugh, she was one of the few club members who lived in my own village. Unfortunately, she travelled by bus so I had no alternative but to do likewise. I developed the habit of waiting for her at the end of the entry to her little terraced house at the far end of the village and seeing her home afterwards, snatching a hurried and clumsy goodnight kiss for my pains in the process. One evening, sensing the time was ripe, and emboldened by the fervour with which my departing kiss was returned, I suggested a date midway through the following week. This was promptly agreed to and although my own preference was for a walk, I settled for the cinema at the nearby town. I arrived home exultant and finding Mother alone and in a more cheerful mood than usual, blurted out the news of my good fortune before blissfully climbing the stairs to bed.

*****************

Hairbrush and comb in hand, I was performing contortions before the kitchen mirror when the bombshell dropped. I had sensed Mother hovering uneasily while Father as usual was hidden from view behind the *Daily Express*. Suddenly, the paper was snatched noisily aside and Father, his voice heavy with foreboding, demanded to know where I was going. Taken aback, I could only stammer 'To meet - a girl.'

'Girl - what girl?' came the demand, harsher than before.

'Father!' The tone of Mother's plea confirmed that a set-to was imminent. As so often in the past, she had fed him the ammunition and was now frantically trying to limit the extent of the damage - in vain.

'Who is she - this - girl?' The last word was spat out like some obscenity. Meekly, through dry lips, I revealed the name I had so proudly given earlier to Mother.

'Shelton!' Ignoring the girl's first name, Father repeated her surname with a boom of contempt. 'No son of mine's being seen with the likes of them!' I tried to plead that

Barbara was a club member, well turned out - all to no avail. Father was adamant.

'Common as muck - all of them!' he thundered. The time had come to play his master card. 'Why - everybody knows her mother's a --!' Despite his anger, he couldn't bring himself to utter the damning word, at least, not in front of an eighteen-year-old innocent. Instead, the implied condemnation of Mrs Sheldon's character hung in the air like a threat, all the more ominous for remaining unsaid.

For a moment, the injustice, the blind unreason of it all, prompted defiance. Mother, sensing this, stepped between us, mumbling something to the effect that Father was doing what he had to do to protect me from the unthinkable. He had, she tried to assure me, my best interests at heart. Impotent in my humiliation, I stormed upstairs to my room and wept bitter tears in the darkness. Later, when the time fixed for my first date had long passed, I groped my way down and put on my old coat and shoes. Mother, seemingly still perplexed at the way things had gone, crept out of the living room and enquired anxiously what I was going to do. Reassured to some extent by my insistence that I was merely taking a short walk, she gripped my sleeve.

'You won't do anything - silly, will you?' she begged. I snatched my arm away and stepped out into the night. Choking back the last remaining sobs, I set off down the lane away from the village - and away from the shame of failing to keep my first date.

Barbara cut my excuses short. To my amazement, she seemed to bear no ill- will and expressed no surprise at my failure to turn up for our date, assuming, she said, that I had had second thoughts on the matter. On reflection, I now realised that what I had taken for her light-hearted references to our differing backgrounds had a deeper significance. She saw me as socially superior to herself and therefore quite within my rights to break a promise. That in itself was bad enough; but for her to accept such a state of affairs without any apparent sign of resentment I found incomprehensible. I had expected anger, scorn, contempt - had indeed felt them to be fully justified. Instead, I was to be denied even the chance to express my regret. It seemed that my shame must remain unuttered and my bitterness pent up within.

At least I had learned a lesson - or rather two. Restrict my amorous activities to villages other than my own and resist the impulse, however tempting, to confide in Mother. The former would be easy enough; the latter would mean breaking the habit of a lifetime. Meanwhile, I went back to cycling to the youth club, where I managed with difficulty to suppress my envy of the youth who promptly and successfully took my place in the pursuit of Barbara, and cast a covetous eye from time to time in the direction of Rita.

For her part, Mother decided that a little guidance in the direction of my social life was called for. From the start, she had let it be known that she disapproved of my belonging to a chapel youth club; now she chanced upon a possible - and in her eyes more respectable - alternative. In conversation with the manageress of the baker's shop in the nearby town, she had learned that the local Conservative association was about to form a youth branch. The woman's son was of about my age and would be joining and I was invited to go along to the first meeting, at which the prospective parliamentary candidate would be present. It would be on a Wednesday evening, Mother pointed out, so avoiding a clash with the youth club. I hesitated. Brought up in a staunch Conservative family, I had accepted unquestioningly Father's political stance - based on *Daily Express* editorials - as a matter of course and was only just beginning, through conversation at work, to appreciate the validity of alternative views. In essence, though, the politics were irrelevant. The question was: would there be girls? Mother applied the decisive push.

'Go along and give it a try,' she coaxed. 'You don't have to join to start with. You won't know what it's like if you don't go.'

\*\*\*\*\*\*\*\*\*\*\*\*\*\*\*\*\*

First impressions were distinctly unfavourable. At Mother's insistence I had caught an early bus and had arrived at the dreary Conservative club building ahead of the official opening time. A gaggle of mature ladies with severely-permed hair turned their questioning gaze at my entrance. One of their number approached me with cautious determination, enquiring the nature of my business. On learning this, the pursed lips blossomed into a beaming smile and I was welcomed into the group

'How nice! Interested in joining the Young Conservatives - how nice!'

Sensing my unease, another lady sought to offer reassurance.

'I'm sure there'll be lots of other young people soon,' she gushed. 'And the candidate - he's so nice. And young too! You'll enjoy meeting him.'

Cornered, I eyed the door anxiously, in the vain hope that others of my own age would appear. But apart from a group of three smirking youths who arrived together and sat at the far end of the hall, the only other persons under forty appeared to be a lean, earnest-looking man with a receding chin and flashing glasses, and a slender, dark-haired girl of about my own age, accompanying a gaudily-dressed woman whom I took to be her mother.

I was wondering how I could possibly extricate myself from this unpromising situation when there was a flurry of

133

excitement in the doorway and a tall, red-faced young man in a dark suit entered, flanked by two others - all three sporting blue rosettes. I was left standing and forgotten as with an ecstatic cry, my captors swept in a body towards the latest attraction, who was ushered to the front of the hall and into a prominent seat at the table.

There followed what for me was an excruciating half-hour or so of incomprehensible speeches interspersed with rounds of applause, after which the candidate was whisked away to another meeting. To the accompaniment of more applause, our pathetic little band of hopefuls was led into an adjoining room by the earnest young man with the flashing glasses. Although small, this room swallowed us up and our self-appointed leader, having established himself at a table at the front, invited us with bleating voice to fill up the front row of seats. The girl and I complied but the sniggering trio opted for the back, from which they vied with one another to interrupt proceedings with a series of inane comments and suggestions, much to the leader's discomfort. At length he declared the meeting closed, having first taken note of our names and addresses. We would, he assured us, hear from him soon, when in response to irresistible public demand, the brand-new branch of the Young Conservatives would be launched.

We left through a side-door as the other meeting was still in progress. The three friends sauntered off noisily into the night. The girl hesitated. Should she wait for Mummy, she pondered aloud, or should she make her own way home? My impulsive offer to walk her there was accepted and by the time we had reached the impressive detached house in a select neighbourhood on the edge of the town, she had told me her name was Dulcie and she had agreed to accompany me to the cinema the following week. With luck, I was about to get myself a girl friend, and one that my parents could hardly fail to approve of - thanks indirectly to the Conservatives.

# Chapter 18

Having set myself, for the time being at any rate, to withhold my latest romantic exploit from Mother, I badly needed to share my glad tidings with someone. My innocence in sexual matters had become a source of harmless amusement at Hallfield, just as at Swainsbrook and elsewhere; and although secretly I derived a certain amount of pleasure from being the centre of attention in this way, I decided that the time had come to reveal that I was about to land my first catch - and an impressive one at that.

And so, in the lamp-room on the following morning, I seized the first opportunity to inform my gentle tormentors of my forthcoming success. Unfortunately, my political naivety matched my sexual innocence and my description of how I had encountered Dulcie at a Conservative meeting met with a mixture of indignation and disbelief. Tories, I was told in forthright terms, were the sworn enemies of miners and as such should be avoided at all costs. As always, however, it took one light-hearted remark to break the tension.

'I wouldna' touch a Tory lass wi' a barge-pole,' one old man pronounced solemnly.

'It's not a bargepole 'e's thinkin' o' usin', is it, m' lad?' came the quick-as-a-flash response from old Jack, the storekeeper, and the man responsible for much of the good-natured teasing to which I was subjected. At this, Ezra, a staunch chapel-goer and in whose workplace we were guests of a kind, asserted his unquestioned authority.

'Now, that'll do, Jack,' he said gravely. 'Gordon 'ere knows how we feel about th' Tories but I'm not 'avin' that sort o' talk in my lamp-room, as well tha' knows.' But old Jack's comment, for all its suggestiveness, had done the trick. I was congratulated, advised to scrub my nails, wash behind my ears and eat my greens - the last by old Jack, who with a wary eye on Ezra, explained with considerable self-restraint that courting was a physically demanding activity that necessitated sensible dietary habits.

At this point, Ezra judged the time had come to wind up the discussion.

'I'm sure that Gordon 'ere'll conduct 'isself properly,' he said, summing up. 'This lass is 'is first gel, so she's rather special.' He paused before adding, 'I'm sure that one day 'e'll find 'isself a really grand Labour lass - an' if she's chapel an' all, then so much th' better.'

The others nodded in agreement. And I thought of Rita.

In fact, I continued to think of Rita - as I had done ever since my futile attempt to persuade her to go out with me - right up to the evening of my date with Dulcie. That event, when it finally arrived, did little to boost my self-confidence. Dulcie, looking neat and alluring, kept me waiting, announced that she preferred the other cinema rather than the one we had agreed on, led me determinedly past the back row, to which I was hopefully attempting to guide her, and when not making disparaging remarks about the happenings on the screen, managed to convey in no uncertain terms that any attempt from me to bridge the gap between our seats would be instantly repelled.

I fared little better on the walk home. The possibility of a bike ride was promptly dismissed; Daddy, I was informed, was about to commence giving driving lessons, with the promise of sharing his car when his darling daughter passed her test. Walks might just be permissible, providing that they were short and confined strictly to pavements .By contrast, dances were very much in favour. Suddenly, Dulcie became animated. She had, it seemed, waltzed from babyhood, while the quickstep was her natural mode of locomotion. And as for the foxtrot – well, that was simplicity itself. I was dismayed. I couldn't dance a step.

It came as something of a surprise when my diffident suggestion of another date, made as we approached the big house in its ample grounds, was accepted - though on condition that I learned to dance in time to accompany Dulcie to the summer ball that her firm would be holding later in the year. A brief goodnight kiss, too, was granted and I set off for home, thankful that what had seemed likely to prove a disastrous evening had not turned out too badly after all. Of course, there was still Mother to face. It was only with difficulty that I had managed to spin a yarn about going with other youths to the pictures. Now I had to maintain the pretence under the scrutiny of her searching questioning. Somehow I came through the ordeal and was even able to broach a subject that had suddenly become vitally important to me.

'We're thinking about having dancing lessons,' I announced, attempting to sound casual. Mother, who had danced herself at one time, registered surprise.

'You've never had a good word to say about dancing before,' she reminded me. I was ready for that.

'No - but I thought it might come in handy when the Young Conservatives get going', I countered.

*****************

The questions came thick and fast in the lamp-room on the following morning. I tried to play down the less-successful aspects of the evening, concentrating instead on Dulcie's attributes and painting a wishful impression of how attuned I was with the enchanting creature that had stepped from the dream world into my life. I was aware that old Jack, under the restraint of Ezra's warning frown, was finding it increasingly difficult to remain silent. At last, when I brought up the subject of dancing, he could hold back no longer and launched into a colourful description of the delights to be had from holding a desirable girl in one's arms - delights which, though hard to achieve in any other situation, were rendered perfectly acceptable when confined to the dance floor.

Ezra, seeking to cut short the old man's salacious monologue, enquired about my own accomplishments as a dancer. Shamefacedly, I had to admit the full extent of my inability. Old Jack needed no further incentive. To my embarrassment, and everyone else's amusement, he was on his feet in an instant, had dragged me with him, and with a lightness of step that belied his years, proceeded to teach me the basic steps of the waltz. The space was limited and the lamp-room floor irregular, in addition to which, old Jack had to dance the lady's steps - and without music, apart, that is, from his own strident humming. Blindly, my cheeks tingling, I stumbled around, trying to obey my teacher's instructions, while at the same time doing my utmost to avoid looking into the creased and stubbly face thrust so disconcertingly close to my own.

At last I was released from the steely grip and, to a ripple of applause, groped my way unsteadily from the miniature improvised dance floor. Old Jack, meanwhile, looking none the worse for his exertions, was talking of giving me another lesson on the following day. I made good my escape and set off down the adit, conscious that Derek, who had witnessed the entire bizarre episode, was still chuckling to himself behind. What Dulcie would have made of my initiation into the world of dance, I couldn't begin to contemplate; she had yet to learn that I worked down a coal mine. And although I wanted desperately to learn to dance, I hoped fervently that old Jack would be struck down overnight with lumbago, or memory loss - or better still, both.

As it happened, the need to become proficient on the dance floor receded as suddenly as it had arisen. I had persuaded Dulcie - very much against her will - to take an evening walk along a quiet road out of the town and back along the towpath of the disused canal. This route, as I well knew, was favoured by courting couples and hopefully would provide the opportunity for me to sample some of the delights that others boasted were there for the taking.

Dulcie, however, had other ideas. For the first mile or so I was made to endure a glowing account of a recent office party, at which she had been the all-too-willing victim of the advances of a suave, half-drunk superior. This was followed by a detailed description of the family's touring holidays, on which, it seemed, every corner of the British Isles worth seeing had been visited, thanks to Daddy and the indispensable Wolseley. My own tally - Skegness and Morecambe, with the youth club's week at Weston-Super-Mare to follow in August - was dismissed with a toss of the head; Weston was common. Daddy wouldn't even stop there.

The canal towpath, though dry and fringed with the burgeoning greenery of spring, did nothing to soften Dulcie's attitude. Apart from reluctantly tolerating my encircling arm, my companion was clearly determined to keep on the move, and my sidelong glances and attempts to slow down at suitable stops for dalliance met with a firm insistence to press on. Apart from Dulcie's uncooperativeness, another cause for concern arose in my mind. I had badly underestimated the time needed to complete the walk. I voiced my fears to Dulcie and suggested we turn back. This idea was rejected outright. On no account would she face that again. We would keep on as far as the nearest bus stop, and the sooner the better. She disengaged and strode on ahead. Meekly, glumly, I followed.

It so happened that the nearest village was that at which I attended the youth club and the bus stop was the one I had used so often on Friday evenings. By now the light was failing; there was no sign of a bus, and Dulcie's patience was at breaking point. She had laddered a stocking climbing a stile and vowed never again to undergo such an ordeal. Just then, I became aware of two figures passing along the pavement opposite. My heart leapt - Rita. Without thinking, I rushed across the road, blurted out my pleasure at seeing her, was introduced to her young brother and bounded back just in time to follow a stony-faced Dulcie on to the bus.

Not a word was spoken and the silence remained unbroken all the way to the garden gate. Dulcie passed through without looking up and my stumbled apology and farewell as she disappeared along the path met with a scarcely audible response. I turned for home, still uninitiated in the wondrous subtleties of sex, yet strangely exhilarated by a heady mixture of relief and – somewhat surprisingly – anticipation.

# Chapter 19

Like the arithmetic tables drilled into me at school, Stanley Holloway's monologues, once learned, were never forgotten. They had lain dormant for several years until one day in the lamp-room, when after someone had embarked on the story of Albert Ramsbottom's fateful visit to the zoo and had dried up in mid-flow, I had taken over and carried the tale through to its conclusion. From that day onwards, my role as impromptu entertainer was assured. I had failed to impress as a dancer and my love life had fizzled out almost before it had begun but here was something I could turn on as easily as a tap. I treated my tiny yet appreciative audience not only to the unlikely adventures of young Albert but also to Sam Small's exploits at Waterloo. Urged on by the clamour for more, I set about extending my repertoire, adding from my book of the complete works The Battle of Hastings, The Magna Carta, and, as proof of my versatility, the tear-jerking Brown Boots.

And as my repertoire grew, so did my confidence. Recalling how Bert Trouncer had embellished his performances with nods, winks and other laughter-inducing mannerisms, I followed suit. My audience, swelled now by others who had invented some reason or other for visiting the lamp-room, responded with ready laughter. Whether or not they were laughing at me or with me I neither knew nor cared; I had an audience - and I loved it.

Then one Friday night at the youth club, a new chance to shine arose. Rain had interrupted our rounders and we had returned to the clubroom, where our leader, obviously unprepared for a change of activity, suggested we concluded the evening with an improvised concert. Reassured after hearing the efforts of other members that I had nothing to lose, I volunteered to recite The Battle of Hastings, in which the conflict between Saxons and Normans is likened to a football match. As most of the youths present were either football players or spectators, the choice was a fortunate one. I exploited the laughter shamelessly, rose to the response, and finished to floor-stamping and thunderous applause.

Back in my seat, flushed with success, I stole a glance at Rita. The smile I received as our eyes met seemed loaded with special significance. Our paths converged as everyone made for the door. Rita came to the point straight away. The chapel would be entering the forthcoming competitive music festival at Nottingham. As well as the usual instrumental and singing sections, there was to be one on elocution. She was to represent the chapel in the female section but no suitable male competitor could be found. Suddenly she seemed much closer. Her eyes, bright and searching, met mine.

'I wondered - would you be prepared to help?' The tone, gently pleading, was irresistible. I promised to attend a meeting at the chapel one evening during the following week.

I hadn't been inside a chapel before. In fact, I hadn't entered a place of worship of any kind since my pleas to be excused from attending church Sunday school had finally been heeded about eight years earlier. I had always thought of chapel folk - if I thought of them at all - as a rather smug and joyless lot, a view promoted by Mother, whose loyalty to the Church of England had doggedly withstood twenty or more years of lapsed membership. Nonconformity, she implied, was an inferior brand of religion and those who practised it, traipsing past the house every week in their Sunday best, were more to be pitied than blamed.

And although the little band of adults who accompanied the youth club to Morecambe had done much to dispel my prejudices, I was still in for an eye-opener. The group of people assembled in the plain little red-brick chapel to tie up the final details for the music festival that evening proved to be both cheerful and friendly. I was welcomed into their midst without a trace of the cloying effusiveness that I had met with in my most recent venture into unfamiliar territory - that dreadful evening at the Conservative club. Even Ron Dobson - sleek and distant on our infrequent encounters at the youth club - threw me a smile of recognition as he slid onto the piano stool to commence the proceedings with a hymn. If he was in any way affected by my close proximity to Rita he showed no sign, nor for that matter did Rita - busily introducing me to her fellow worshippers - reveal any special interest in him.

An hour or so later, a full list of competitors had been drawn up and test pieces distributed. I was to render Tennyson's *The Brook*, vaguely recalled from school days and a far cry from Albert and the Lion. It was dusk as, pushing my bike, I escorted Rita to her home, one of a row of terraced cottages, each with a tunnel-like rear entry similar to that outside which I had bid lingering farewells to Barbara. I stifled the thought.

Rita's face peered up at mine in the half-light. 'I used to love bike rides,' she confided. 'Haven't been on one for ages, though.' My heart missed a beat. 'I've asked Dad to check my bike over - it's nowhere near as flash as yours.' I mumbled something conciliatory. 'I expect your girl friend's bike's one of those posh ones with -.'

I hastened to clarify things. 'I haven't got a girl friend – now,' I blurted. 'It's over. We finished – the night I saw you.'

The goodnight kiss, when it finally came, was all the sweeter for the waiting. I returned the wave from the shadows and pedalled homeward, giving full voice to every love song I could think of. The prospect of bike rides, walks – and kisses – was almost too delicious to contemplate.

I couldn't wait to share my good news with my friends in the lamp-room. After having to play down my brief and disastrous relationship with Dulcie, I could now let it be known that I was the proud possessor, not only of a girl friend, but of a vivacious, chapel-going - and in time no doubt, Labour-voting - girl friend at that. The response was all that I could have wished for. Back-slapping and hand-shaking was followed by polite and tactful enquiries about Rita's background, employment and appearance, the colliery at which her father worked, and - from Ezra - whether I intended becoming a member of the chapel.

As before, however, old Jack came to the rescue just as the going began to get difficult. After his initial offer to provide me with what he called 'a packet-of-three' had been ruled out of order by the ever-vigilant Ezra, he switched subject to bike rides, which, I had already intimated, would be one of our future evening activities. In his own youthful biking days, he recalled with pleasure, he had discovered a quiet lane midway between Hallfield and my own village which skirted the foot of the common overlooking the Amber valley. It was on this hilltop, he went on with a chuckle, that he later courted his future wife and which, he assured me, still remained the ideal place for lingering lovers.

At this point, Ezra decided that enough was enough. ''Th' lad's quite capable o' findin' 'is own courtin' places,' he reminded Jack, '-wi'out 'avin' t' rely on such as thee t' tell 'im where t' go.' How right he was; in fact I had already begun to reappraise the potential of some of my favourite local haunts from an entirely new perspective.

It was on one of our early walks that I learned that Rita's mother was friendly with a distant relative of Mother's. And although she and Mother seldom met, I realised that sooner or later I would need to let it be known at home that I had a girl friend. I had already announced that I would be entering the elocution section of the music festival, which because I had made it appear to be on behalf of the youth club, had been accepted without comment. I decided to adopt a similar line over Rita, omitting any mention of chapel. It now remained only to choose an appropriate time to break the news.

I had been working steadily at my correspondence course and my tutor's comments, somewhat guarded to begin with, were by now distinctly encouraging. I had formed the habit of reading these comments to my parents as we sat around the kitchen table and after one particularly glowing verdict on an article on natural history, which had been received with grunts of satisfaction, I decided the time was ripe - or as ripe as it would ever be. Even so, my news was greeted with a silence that hardly boded well for the future. I tried to pass the matter off lightly, referring to Rita by her first name only but Father was having none of it. In trepidation I at last revealed her surname, fearful that by some unhappy quirk of fate he would know something scandalous about this family too, even though they lived in a village three miles away. To my relief, however, no such revelation followed. In answer to further questioning, I was compelled to reveal that Rita worked in a hosiery factory and that her father was a miner. Mother's dismay was expressed in a telling sigh. Father returned to his *Daily Express*.

Not counting Friday evenings at the youth club, our meetings were confined by mutual consent to twice weekly. They were spent either walking over the local field paths or biking along the few quiet country lanes within easy distance of Rita's home. To begin with, and despite having to travel to Rita's village by bus, I preferred the walks. The lane leading down to the old canal, along which I had hurried with Dulcie on our one and only country excursion, was only a short distance from Rita's home and the restraint which she exercised as we set off was soon relaxed as we left the last of the houses behind. Our favourite lingering place was beneath a gnarled old oak tree standing on a low mound by a hedgerow just off the path. Here, by pressing ourselves close to the far side of the mighty trunk, we were virtually invisible to anyone passing. One evening, we found to our dismay that our chosen spot was already occupied. Unaware of our approach, the usurpers were clearly in no hurry to move and judging by their grunts and groans, their degree of intimacy was far in excess of anything we had experienced. Averting our eyes, we passed by, in the vain hope of finding another secluded place further on.

Later, on our way back, a mixture of curiosity and foreboding prompted us to veer from the path towards our familiar tree. The couple had gone, but as well as littering the place with cigarette ends and sweet wrappers, they had left behind, impaled on a nearby thorn, a telltale reminder of the frenetic activity they had engaged in earlier. Rita tugged at my arm.

'Let's go,' she whispered, her voice thick with disgust. I needed no further bidding. My own desire, though unfulfilled, had ebbed away without trace.

# Chapter 20

There was an air of expectancy in the lamp-room. It had been clear for some time that all was far from well at Ezra's chapel; a new minister had been appointed and the abrasive way in which he had set about implementing changes in long-established tradition had deeply offended a number of the elders, Ezra included. Matters had come to a head as spring advanced and a meeting had been arranged in an attempt to resolve the difficulties. This was to take place over the weekend, which meant that we wouldn't know the outcome until the following Monday and by the time that morning arrived, excitement, though respectfully muted, was nevertheless in the air.

Ezra related the weekend's events in solemn tones. It appeared that the meeting intended to put matters right had ended in failure. A few waverers had decided reluctantly to abide by the changes but the majority, led by Ezra himself, had flatly refused to accept the new minister's dictates and had walked out of the meeting in protest. But the matter hadn't ended there. We sat in silence as Ezra went on to relate in a voice wavering with emotion how on Sunday morning he had led his family with sombre and deliberate steps past the chapel in which they had worshipped for a lifetime and on to another of a different denomination at the opposite end of the village.

Having heard the momentous news, we dispersed with lowered voices, soberly conscious that we had been privileged to hear at first hand of an important event in the life of a respected member of the colliery community. Never one to allow a cloud of gloom to hover for long over proceedings, old Jack was back to his usual self by the time I returned to the lamp-room at the end of my shift. A discussion was under way on the subject of the employment of women and children underground; apparently someone had asserted that this practice had continued in the Hallfield locality long after the passing of legislation to bring it to an end. This was the cue for old Jack to intervene.

'There were an owd woman livin' at th' end o' our row when I were a lad,' he began in sonorous tones, '- an' o' allus said that o' were got in th' pit.'

Hoots of disbelief greeted this assertion but old Jack stuck determinedly to his story, while at the same time directing an outsize wink towards Derek and me. I did a quick calculation; bearing in mind that the law was passed in the 1840s and that judging by his appearance, old Jack was then about sixty, his story could well have been true.

It was at about this time that my assistant linesman began bringing gifts for me from the smallholding he farmed with his father. The occasional duck egg gave place to a box of fresh hens' eggs, which I bore home proudly to Mother. Her initial reluctance to accept what she saw as charity was eventually defused when I managed to press the appropriate payment into Derek's hand. One spring afternoon, as we finished work, Derek shyly suggested that I accompany him to see the family smallholding. The weather being fine, I had taken to biking to work so with no bus to catch, I accepted readily. Though not far from the pit, the holding was set in unspoilt countryside close to the family's cottage. As he led me proudly round the couple of hedged fields, with their scattering of hen coops and pigsties, I saw a new Derek emerge. The gawky, diffident youth disappeared, to be replaced by a mature and confident young man, happily and purposefully absorbed in a world of farming - his natural calling. The pit, and all it represented, suddenly seemed a hundred miles away.

It so happened that Derek's smallholding lay close to the hilltop common that old Jack had recommended I visit in the course of my courting exploits and so I decided to cycle home that way. Sure enough, the steep, gorse-clad slopes, high above a quiet lane, looked ideal for the purpose. We could hide our bikes in the roadside bushes, scale the low wall, and disappear from view amid the luxuriant gorse, with no fear of our hiding place being detected, let alone defiled by others.

And so, as the spring days lengthened, our twice-weekly evening meetings took the form of bike rides, more often than not in the direction of the common. We soon discovered a good hiding place for our bikes, with a convenient gap in the wall nearby, and an ill-defined yet easily traceable path, which wriggled its way up between the bushes to the rim of an old quarry high on the hillside.

One timeless evening, as we lay absorbed in our newly-discovered pleasures, with only the twittering linnets for company, we became vaguely aware of the splutter and cutting-out of a motor bike engine on the lane below. We were accustomed to the drone of the occasional passing vehicle but this was the first time that our peace had been disturbed in this way. We waited, hoping, expecting to hear the engine restart but when, after some considerable time all remained silent, we began to feel uneasy and I decided to investigate. Getting to my feet, I peered   between the bushes and down the descending path.  Apart from us, the hillside appeared deserted. However, I could just make out a metallic glint under a roadside tree not far from the spot where our bikes were hidden and after a whispered discussion, we decided it was time to go. Back on the lane, we were relieved to find our bikes exactly as we had left them. However, parked nearby was an unattended motor bike, which I recognised immediately as belonging to old Jack, the colliery store-keeper. Could it just be, I pondered as we cycled homeward, that pure chance had brought the old man back to his courting haunts of yesteryear? Or had his hidden presence a less excusable motive? I had heard that some old men made a habit of spying on courting couples; was old Jack one of their number, and if so, was it mere coincidence that we were on the common at the same time, or had the wily old fox guessed that I would take his advice and bring Rita there? Perhaps the time had come to seek a new hideaway.

*****************

To my amazement, I came third in the elocution section at the music festival. This modest success bore fruit almost immediately. I was invited to Rita's home for tea, introduced to various members of her family, and asked to join a concert party about to be formed to entertain local pensioners' groups. Suddenly, for the first time in my life, I found myself called upon to balance a full social life with the demands of work and study - a state of affairs which did wonders for my self-confidence. At my tutor's suggestion, I had chosen the twin fields of natural history and the countryside in which to specialise on my correspondence course and I decided to submit a sample of my work to the editor of the local weekly newspaper. As luck would have it, the long-term contributor of a country column had just relinquished the task and I was promptly appointed as his successor at the rate of a penny-halfpenny a line. This was on the understanding that, unlike those of my much- respected predecessor, to begin with my contributions would be included only when space permitted, but with the possibility of a regular column if my style proved popular with the readership.

Father received the news of my forthcoming breakthrough into print with gratifying satisfaction. He had long since ceased to read my predecessor's pieces on the grounds that his rambling style was too gossipy for his taste.

'You've got to begin somewhere,' he pronounced. 'And if you can't do any better than that old codger, you've no business calling yourself a writer.'

Mother, however, was far from happy. Ever since Father had had a minor brush with the law some years before, which had been faithfully reported in the paper, she had harboured a dread of seeing the family name in print. And that fear gave rise to others.

'But if they print your name and something you write turns out to be wrong - then what happens?' she speculated miserably. In the end, it was only with serious misgivings that she agreed to my pieces appearing - and then under my initials rather than my name.

How this contrasted with the breaking of my news in the lamp-room! Without exception, everybody expressed delight at my success. Following the incident involving the motor bike on the common, I had kept a wary eye on old Jack, half-expecting him to make some allusion to the evening in question but none had been forthcoming. Now, however, boldly ignoring Ezra's warning stare, he proffered me his services in writing about the love-life of the birds and bees - an offer which Ezra was quick to decline on my behalf.

The highlight of my working week was the visit of my immediate superior, Walter Thorne. A quietly-spoken, bespectacled bachelor, Walter was totally unlike any of the other young men I encountered during my mining days. Like me, he had drifted into colliery surveying almost by chance, and although seemingly contented with his lot, I suspected that this was rendered tolerable by his range of outside interests. Thanks to Walter, I was now gaining immense pleasure from listening to classical music, while as a result of another discussion on a lengthy journey underground, I was prompted to buy the first of many Bartholomew half-inch maps, and in so doing discover the delights of planning cycle trips into the Peak District.

Walter's reserved and outwardly serious disposition proved something of a mystery to the regulars in the lamp-room. I learned that before my arrival, some of the men, led by old Jack, had attempted in vain to ferret out details of his home life. Even now, the odd query concerning possible romantic attachments was made from time to time. However, Walter refused to rise to the bait and apart from the occasional suggestive remark, he was allowed to come and go undisturbed.

It was a different story in the area office, however. Although I was present only on Saturday mornings, I was conscious of a good deal of chaffing, most of it good-natured, and chiefly relating to Walter's dress sense - or rather, lack of it. For despite being quite well paid, he wore the same drab, army-surplus type clothing throughout the year and this, together with his frugal lifestyle generally, earned him a reputation for meanness to which he appeared indifferent, and which, as I was to discover later, was completely unjustified.

In the meantime, my working life at Hallfield went on smoothly and uneventfully. Until, that is, a message awaited my return to the surface one day, informing me that as from the new year, I would be transferred to a larger colliery closer to home.

# Chapter 21

My second seaside holiday with the youth club, at Weston-super-Mare, was a rip-roaring success. Des - by now totally immersed in courting - had long since ceased to be a member; I was surrounded by familiar faces and most important of all, I had my girl friend with me. A group of us, the nucleus of the newly-formed concert party, decided to enter a talent competition held at the seafront bandstand and to my amazement, my rendering of Albert and the Lion was awarded a special prize - a visit to a studio at which the monologue was recorded. The fact that we didn't possess a gramophone seemed of little consequence at the time.

Back home, Mother announced that as my now regular visits to Rita's home seemed to indicate that we were 'going serious', the time had come when she should be invited over for tea. A date was fixed and I awaited its coming with trepidation. How would Rita react to my parents' critical scrutiny? Would Mother come out with one of her anti-chapel outbursts? Worse still, would Father don his *Daily Express* crusader's mantle and give vent to his customary wrath against all things even remotely associated with the Labour government?

As it turned out, these fears proved groundless. Mother, having spared no effort in preparing an extra special tea, served on her Sunday-best crockery, was clearly out to demonstrate her seldom-exercised accomplishments as a hostess; Father, meanwhile, had washed, shaved and donned a clean shirt for the occasion and was at his most bluff and genial. In fact, the only minor ripples to disturb the otherwise tranquil nature of the event were of Rita's making; I could only look on in silent admiration as, far from being overawed by the occasion, she chatted away with no hint of self-consciousness, volunteering her opinions in the same forthright manner as was normal in her own family situation.

Later, on returning from seeing her home, I sensed immediately that the visit had been well and truly discussed during my absence. And it was all too apparent that Mother, for all her solicitousness at the time, had formed a distinct impression of my girl-friend and that this impression was not entirely favourable.

'Plenty to say for herself, that's for sure,' she commented dryly. 'Talk about the gift of the gab! My word, there's no mistaking she's a chapelite. Stands out a mile.'

Father, by contrast, was conciliatory. 'She seemed a nice enough lass. I expect she was a bit nervous. It was only to be expected when you come to think about it.'

Mother, however, was unconvinced. 'I didn't see much sign of nerves. In fact, I had a job getting a word in edgeways while we were washing up.'

Stung by this, I pointed out that Rita came from a large family and that lively discussion was just as natural in her home as brooding silence was in ours. '-And I know which I prefer!' I blurted angrily as I made for the door.

Quick as a flash, Mother managed to fire her last telling barb before I could stomp off upstairs. 'Well, if you're satisfied with a factory girl, then that's up to you.'

\*\*\*\*\*\*\*\*\*\*\*\*\*\*\*\*

That autumn, I added yet another activity to my already overcrowded evenings. At Walter's suggestion, I joined a local history class of which he was already a member and which was held in a nearby secondary school. The tutor was the school's history master - in appearance a slight, unprepossessing man approaching retirement but born and bred in the area and widely recognised as the leading authority on its chequered past. Under this remarkable man's tutelage, history - and especially local history - suddenly became an exciting subject. The dry-as-dust clutter of history as I had hitherto known it - kings' reigns, dates of battles and treaties - was banished to the sidelines in favour of a colourful and compelling account of the lives of the men and women, across the social scale, all of whom had helped make our corner of England what it was. We studied maps, family trees, original documents; we learnt of feats of daring and inventiveness; of villainous acts and scandalous deeds. Through the almost childlike enthusiasm and modest erudition of this man, I and no doubt countless others of his students began to see our surroundings in an entirely new and revealing light.

The onset of winter meant that evening bike rides had to be discontinued. And in any case, we had failed to find a suitable substitute for the common. And despite all my pleadings, weekend rides, Rita insisted, were out of the question - home commitments on Saturday and chapel on Sunday saw to that. Nor could I persuade her to join the local history class, which meant that our meetings were restricted to a weekly evening walk, weather permitting, and rehearsals and performances of the concert party.

An unhappy evening at the fun fair in the local town marked the end of my first romance. I had been reluctant to go in the first place, preferring our usual walk. Rita, however, had insisted, with the result that I had indulged in one of my increasingly frequent black moods. Harsh words were exchanged and our parting at the entry-end was abrupt and final. Thereafter, our infrequent encounters at the youth club were coolly polite, while my involvement in the concert party was soon to terminate in favour of a new 'career' in amateur dramatics.

\*\*\*\*\*\*\*\*\*\*\*\*\*\*\*\*

Leaving Hallfield Colliery was made easier for me by a change of management. The elderly manager retired shortly before my transfer and his place was taken by a quick-tempered young official of the new-broom mould, who in his eagerness to make his mark wasted no time in asserting his influence both on the surface and underground. He was in the habit of bursting into the lamp-room without warning and demanding to know the reason why others, apart from the two attendants, were present. He confronted me early on, and being unable to find anything amiss, made a point of saying that my equipment should not be stored on the premises and that he would find me an alternative place. I was told that he had come down especially hard on old Jack, after having found the store unmanned and discovered the storekeeper in full flow in the lamp-room. For once, the old man had been reduced to cowed silence and all I saw of him as I worked out my time was the pale, bespectacled face, topped by the flat cap, peering out forlornly from the storeroom window.

My farewell, when it came, was a low-key affair. I'd miss Derek, my warm-natured assistant, and the friendliness of all the men I worked with. But most of all I'd miss Ezra, a Christian gentleman whose quiet dignity shone through the grime and grimness of colliery life. My parents welcomed the move as promotion, whereas in fact it was no such thing. My weekly wage remained at seven pounds ten shillings and although my journey to work was shorter, as the colliery was considerably larger than Hallfield the workload was correspondingly greater. To Mother, however, the chief cause for rejoicing was that I would once again be able to use pit-head baths and she would no longer have to face the indignity of seeing her son come through the gate in his pit dirt.

Mrs Fairbrother, having heard from Father about my

impending transfer, lost no time in making her view known. 'On no account let this affect your writing,' she declared. 'You must not lose sight of your main aim - to prepare for your new career, ready for when you can leave the mines.' To my disappointment, she was unimpressed by my breakthrough into print in the local paper. 'That's merely a first step - and an over-cautious one at that,' she pronounced. 'Aim high. Always aim high. Never settle for the second-rate.'

She had nothing but contempt for Mother's insistence on my work appearing under my initials. 'Poppycock!' she scoffed. 'Any editor worth his salt would have insisted on printing your full name. The sooner it appears in print, the better.' She had heard, too, of my attendance at a local history class. 'That should provide you with ideas for articles. The county magazine will do for a start. Remember - aim high!'

The youth club, which had been instrumental in opening up my sheltered little world, had one last - and lasting - benefit to bestow before we finally parted company . Margaret, my new girl friend - slight, dark, neat - and to begin with, engagingly shy- was over three years my junior and our association soon led to good-natured accusations of cradle-snatching from other youths. Like Rita, she came from a mining family but worked in an office and, to my relief, her church and family ties, though strong, didn't present the obstacle that I had encountered previously. She also shared an interest in drama; had a bike; and expressed a willingness to join me in my intended explorations of the Peak District in the following spring. All in all, 1950 promised to be an interesting year.

# Chapter 22

To begin with, however, my energies were directed towards my new post. Asherton Colliery lay on the edge of the nearby market town, in what was once gentle pastoral country, drained by an alder-fringed brook, a tributary of the River Amber. One of two large mines formerly owned by a prosperous private company, it had opened in late Victorian times but had been extensively modernised and had its own 'model' village close by, together with a superior and discreetly-sited manager's house. It had a strong sporting tradition - for cricket especially - and with considerable reserves of coal as yet untapped, its future appeared bright.

I already knew the unit surveyor, Tim Woolley, and his assistant, through my Saturday mornings at area office, and found them both pleasant and helpful, though I knew that I should indeed be fortunate to find such a congenial bunch of men at this colliery as I'd known at Hallfield. Compared with the other pits I'd experienced, Asherton was an up-to-date, efficiently run outfit. The substantial office block, in one corner of which my equipment was stored, overlooked a spacious yard, beyond which the workshops, boilers, screening plant, lamp-room, canteen, baths and medical centre were set out around the twin shafts, the headstocks of which, together with the tall, tapering chimney, dominated the scene.

Most impressive of all was the sense of order that prevailed everywhere. Whereas at other pits I had known, clutter in every imaginable form had been the norm, here tidiness was evidently the watchword. I soon encountered the reason for this in the presence of the manager, Mr B.R. Jefferson. Short and stocky, bull-necked and florid-faced, B. R. Jefferson was the only colliery manager in the area to have retained his post from pre-nationalisation days. A public-school educated Northumbrian, he had, I gathered, been drafted in by the owners in pre-war years to save a failing pit and with a blend of managerial skill and fearless determination had transformed Asherton's fortunes so dramatically that not even the Coal Board's most influential new bosses saw fit to challenge his omnipotence.

BRJ, I soon learned, was a man of moods. The prevailing mood was one of uneasy calm, during which those who came into contact with him trod on tiptoe, communicated in whispers, and generally lived in fear of the next outburst, which could occur without any apparent warning. Like the behaviour of a notorious volcano, BRJ's past eruptions gave rise to countless tales - a whole folklore which included memorable examples of his violence over the years. Some of these stories related to his time as commanding officer of the colliery's Home Guard platoon, in which his displays of temper, according to all accounts, would have made those of Captain Mainwaring in *Dad's Army* seem timid by comparison. Even the miners' union officials - who under the new order benefited from a greatly enhanced status - approached the manager's office with caution. There was a good deal of clearing of throats and removing of caps and helmets before the hesitant tap on the door, followed by deferential mumbles of apology for intruding as they responded to the barked command from within.

Occasionally - very occasionally - BRJ revealed another and contrasting facet of his nature. He was said to fling open the connecting doors of his office with those of his clerk and the time-office staff to regale everyone within earshot with some coarse joke he had come across, following which his audience were duty-bound to add their appreciative laughter to his own thunderous bellow. It was generally assumed that these all-too-rare outbursts of good humour were directly related to certain indulgences granted on the previous night by Mrs Jefferson, and the wish was often fervently expressed that she would in future offer these comforts on a more frequent basis.

It so happened that the cupboards reserved for survey equipment were situated in a small room next to Mr Jefferson's office. This contained the telephone switchboard, manned by a disabled miner, Larry, who welcomed me and my newly-appointed assistant, Neville, with an effusiveness that we both found somewhat embarrassing. We learned that Larry, who had lost an arm in a pit-cage accident, was a bachelor and a devout churchman, and possessed a fine tenor voice. It was only later, and after unwittingly allowing ourselves at different times to be alone in his company, that we discovered to our cost that not only was he prone to inflicting his faith on the unsuspecting, but given the opportunity he could use the fingers of his one arm to decidedly unpleasant effect. Thereafter, we made a point of keeping our encounters with him as brief and distant as possible.

Although my work underground was exactly the same as at Hallfield, conditions at Asherton were infinitely more congenial. The mine was virtually dry throughout and the workings, though deep, were generally well ventilated. Despite the inevitable subsidence resulting from modern methods of extraction, the roadways, being regularly maintained, were easy to travel. The main disadvantage as far as we were concerned was that because this was a shaft mine, we were unable to walk out after completing our work but had to persuade a sometimes reluctant official to interrupt coal-winding to allow us back to the surface. On one occasion, soon after taking up my duties, we reached the pit bottom just as the cage was being made ready for Mr Jefferson to ascend. He gave us a stony stare as we made to follow him on board and the silence of the upward journey was broken only by a resonant belch, causing young Neville to give way to a fit of nervous giggling, which he fought desperately hard, though without much success, to suppress.

Compared with their superior, the two under-managers were much less formidable characters. Mr Potts, the elder of the two, was a genial giant of a man, whose hulking frame shook with wheezy laughter at his every jest, and they were many. I soon learned not to sit by his side in the pit-bottom office, as his every witticism was accompanied by a rib-jarring poke from his mighty elbows. He lived some distance from the colliery and drove to work in an ancient, immaculately-maintained Hillman, reputedly given to him by his father-in-law as a wedding present - according to its owner, in gratitude for taking the old man's daughter off his hands. Potts was said to have two beautiful daughters of his own, who, like their mother, were devout churchgoers, whereas Potts himself, when not engaged in tinkering with his car, preferred to spend his leisure hours raising sweet peas in his garden.

His fellow under-manager, Mr Barber, had - he never tired of reminding everyone - attained his position through blood, sweat and tears. Beginning in the pit as a pony-ganger, he had struggled through night school to gain his qualifications and still had difficulty with basic spelling and grammar. He kept a tatty pocket dictionary handy when completing his report sheets and mouthed every word as he dragged his pencil laboriously across the page. Promotion had enabled him to buy a caravan and he devoted every holiday to touring Devon and Cornwall, where allegedly his meek little wife spent her time knitting while Barber himself indulged in his favourite occupation of eyeing swimsuit-clad girls from his seafront vantage point.

Before my transfer to Asherton I had never been called upon to work night shifts. Now, however, things were about

162

to change. Tim Woolley proposed to carry out a detailed survey of a newly-developed section of the pit and for various reasons this could only be achieved after coal-getting had been completed. This meant that intermittently over a period of several weeks we would be descending at ten o'clock in the evening and surfacing in time for breakfast, round about dawn. This change of routine was hard to adjust to at first, chiefly because the switch-over occurred only occasionally. Though tired, I found sleep difficult during daylight and as spring advanced, was lured from my bed to cycle off into the Peak foothills to enjoy the peace and scenery in the absence of weekend traffic.

It was on one such afternoon that, leaning over the handrail of a footbridge spanning the River Amber, I experienced the never-to-be-forgotten thrill of seeing a tiny arrow of iridescent blue speed from beneath my feet to disappear round a tree-fringed bend ahead - my first kingfisher. This chance encounter was to prove of lasting significance as a hitherto dormant love of nature began its long-overdue awakening, to provide a lifetime's delight.

Working occasional nights enabled me to meet a race of men that I wouldn't otherwise have encountered - the regular night shift. More often than not elderly or in some way unfit to undertake more strenuous work, these men were not merely resigned to their lot but often preferred their nocturnal routine to days or afternoons.

'Gerrin' away from th' missis,' was often given as a reason for this preference, although judging by their reluctance to elaborate, I suspect that this was something of a knee-jerk response. Certainly, Mr Jefferson's absence was a distinct bonus to some; in fact it soon became clear that the comparatively leisurely tempo of night-shift work served to compensate many of these men for the unsocial hours.

One such man was Billy, whose job it was to clear away

roof falls in one of the roadways along which we frequently passed. We were in the habit of teasing Billy about leaving his wife alone in the house with their lodger, a young Latvian-born mining student, whom we happened to know. One night, however, Billy failed to respond to our banter and it was clear that something was troubling him. On enquiring, we discovered that while cleaning the young man's room, Billy's wife had found a camera and a number of maps open on his bed. We were aware that the Latvian was a keen cyclist and photographer and assured Billy that his activities were quite harmless. However, the old man remained far from convinced and declared his belief that his lodger was a Russian spy and that he wouldn't rest until he had got rid of him. Sure enough, we heard later that Billy and his wife had made life so uncomfortable for the young man that he had found accommodation elsewhere.

Another elderly man we came across, a veteran of the Great War and a staunch patriot, confided in us his belief that Germany and the United States were plotting together to secure world domination. When asked to elaborate, he drew our attention to the similarity in the names of the leaders - Adenauer and Eisenhower - of the two countries in question. This resemblance, he insisted, was no mere coincidence; the two villains were obviously related and it was only a matter of time before they made their wicked move. In that case, we replied, we'd better hurry back to the surface without delay, to persuade BRJ to reconvene the Home Guard.

# Chapter 23

It was through a member of the concert party that Margaret and I severed our links with the group, and ultimately with the youth club. Our informant was responsible for the lighting of one of the two leading miners' welfare amateur dramatic societies in the area and happened to mention that casting for the next production was about to take place and that the producer was particularly keen to audition young actors. He had, he said, mentioned our names.

I, for one, needed no second bidding. I had already seen one of the society's productions, performed before a packed and appreciative audience in the spacious and well-equipped theatre, and the prospect of participating in such a world held an irresistible appeal. A further incentive, though hardly needed, was the fact that the leading actor in the rival drama group a few miles distant was none other than H.L. Wilkes, the area chief surveyor who had appointed me over two years earlier. The two societies never failed to attend each other's productions and even though, in the unlikely event that Mr Wilkes remembered me, my emergence as a fellow thespian could have no bearing on my future in the industry, it would be extremely satisfying to be seen to have succeeded in something, and to have my name - not merely my initials - in print, on a play programme.

The producer, a portly and pompous insurance agent, wasted no time in letting us know that any ideas we may have entertained that parts were there for the taking were sadly misplaced. He produced plays, he informed us, to a professional standard. His aim was to bring theatre - real quality theatre - to this cultural backwater. He conceded that, for many in the audience, what took place on the stage was merely entertainment - a night out 'up at the welfare' - but he remained undeterred. The society's reputation was firmly established and the number of discerning theatre-goers was growing, some coming from far afield. He had already a talented and enthusiastic band of actors drawn from all walks of life but he was always on the lookout for new blood. Now, would we measure up to the standard he demanded? He would, he said, soon find out.

We were given copies of a script and invited to join a reading circle, in which I immediately recognised the faces of actors I had seen performing in the last production. Without exception, everyone seemed to read with fluency and polish, as though they had already mastered their parts. I read ahead anxiously, fearful of missing my cue when my chance came. This was no happy-go-lucky concert party rehearsal - this was the big time and we had to prove ourselves equal to it. The session over, the others broke into chatty little groups and made for the bar; the producer, however, his face inscrutable, loomed before us. So far so good, he conceded. We were at the raw material stage, of course - very raw, in fact. But if we'd care to come to next week's pre-casting rehearsal, he'd see how we fared on the stage. That would be the real test. Yes, we assured him, we would.

How right he was. Trying to comply with directions boomed from the semi-darkness of the auditorium below, while at the same time attempting to read and interpret an unfamiliar script proved a nerve-wracking experience, especially as the other actors seemed to combine these activities with ease. A few whispered words of encouragement from them helped to offset the producer's caustic tone, however, and eventually things began to fit into place and we found ourselves warming to the task. Nevertheless, it came as a pleasant surprise to learn at the end of the evening that we had both landed parts in the spring production, rehearsals of which were to commence on a twice-weekly basis straight away.

It was fortunate that I had almost completed my journalism course; otherwise it would have been difficult to fit drama into what had become a crowded evening schedule. I was still getting a great deal out of the local history class; my pieces in the local paper were appearing - still under my initials - almost weekly, and largely through Mrs Fairbrother's promptings, I was beginning to assemble a quantity of material, culled from various sources that would, I hoped, prove useful in my future writing. This included cuttings from the *Manchester Guardian*, carefully dated and classified, copies of the county magazine, and notes made from books borrowed from Mrs Fairbrother and from the library in the nearby town. As yet, I possessed very few books of my own but thanks to the chance discovery in Nottingham of a second-hand bookshop, I began to build my own library, confined at first to volumes on Derbyshire and the English countryside in general, but soon expanding to include books on all branches of natural history, especially insects and birds.

In short, I'd only a vague idea of where I was going, but at least the journey was proving more and more absorbing.

*******************

Our first weekend bike ride was a disaster. I had planned a 30-mile ride in the Wirksworth - Ashbourne area, which with a whole day to complete seemed well within our capabilities. However, the scattered April showers promised in the weather forecast gave way early on to a continuous downpour; capes and leggings donned as a novelty became an uncomfortable hindrance. Soggy sandwiches eaten in a barn doorway did little to lift the spirits and it was not until we were well on the way homeward that the rain relented and allowed watery sunshine to bring brief consolation. Peeling off our saturated rainwear, it occurred to us that our time might have been better spent perfecting our lines for the play, which was looming close by now. In future, I promised, I'd await a dry spell before suggesting another long-distance ride. In the meantime we determined to give the play our undivided attention.

Which was just as well. For as the production date drew close and the play took over our lives, it was brought home to us what a world of difference there was between performing a few light-hearted sketches before an uncritical gathering of old folk and interpreting a role in a full-length play before a packed audience, including the local press. I was also aware that several members of the survey department - including Lionel, my former Swainsbrook workmate - intended being present, as well as a sizeable contingent from our rival society. Would that include the celebrated H.L. Wilkes, I wondered? And if so, was there the faintest hope that he would recall interviewing the nervous youth playing the part of a poised and polished young man-of-the-world ?

I never did find out the answer to that question. But what I did discover - as everyone who has trod the boards knows - was the powerful thrill of helping to create an imaginary world for an appreciative audience, who for a couple of hours allow themselves to be carried away from the reality of everyday life and at the end of it all reward those responsible with rapturous applause. I learned later that during one scene, in which the villain of the piece, a ruthlessly ambitious woman, revealed a particularly nasty streak of her nature, a woman in the audience was so carried away by the actress's portrayal that she blurted out 'You hateful bitch, you!' before shrinking back into her seat in shame.

The play's successful four-night run over, it was a pleasant surprise to find that there were other rewards yet to come. Complimentary press reviews made welcome reading; even Mother managed to forget her distaste for publicity and allowed Father to read excerpts to her. More satisfying still was learning how many of the men I worked alongside, apart from survey staff, came along, together with their wives. For days afterwards, men I scarcely knew would stop me as I passed their workplace, more often than not to tease me about the embracing and kissing that had taken place - all of which in my youthful conceit I relished. One old man in particular returned again and again to the subject of the love scenes, wondering if, as in his army days, a little something was added to my tea to control my passion. This led me to speculate how old Jack, the storekeeper at Hallfield, would have reacted at seeing me in this unaccustomed role. I suspect that Ezra would have had to intervene in his sternest manner to stem the flow of choice observations on the delights and dangers of appearing on the stage.

# Chapter 24

With the play over and spring's promise daily becoming a reality, I determined to savour every available moment in the open air. I reached the surface by 2.30 on most afternoons, having already heard what the weather was like 'on top' from some official coming down early for the afternoon shift. Stepping from the cage into the fresh air of a spring afternoon was a sensation the like of which I have never since experienced. I aimed to have showered, changed and be pedalling into the country by 3 o'clock, my destination varying according to the weather and to the arduousness of my day's labours. On a day when my work took me into part of the pit where conditions were reasonably good, I would complete a delightful circular ride, say through Oakerthorpe, South Wingfield, Crich and Pentrich, stopping at intervals to admire the view, speculate on various features of the landscape that caught my eye, or merely to soak in the atmosphere around me; near, yet seemingly so very far, from the raw, dehumanised world of the coalfield.

On one such timeless afternoon, I discovered a sunken lane climbing between blackened gritstone walls towards a wooded horizon. Nearing the brow, my attention was drawn to a ruined building half-visible over the wall, which proved to be the crumbling remains of an old windmill, perched on its tiny knoll and commanding superb views over the Amber valley. This secret hollow ruin became a place of pilgrimage almost, reached with satisfaction and departed from with regret. Never once was my solitude at this spot disturbed; I rejoiced in having soaring larks as sole companions, while at my feet tiny harebells trembled in the playful breeze.

For every comparatively easy day's work, however, a shift spent trudging several miles, burdened by heavy equipment, or crawling along low coal faces through dust and fumes, left me too weary to tackle such demanding exercise. On these afternoons, the most I could manage was a short ride into the nearest stretch of the Amber valley. Since my chance sighting of the kingfisher, however, this option brought its own rewards, for I began to learn the discipline of patient observation, usually from the parapet of a bridge, and this activity - or more accurately, inactivity - led in time to an appreciation of the natural world that has sustained me ever since.

I was lingering on the footbridge from which I had seen the kingfisher one afternoon when a slight movement along the trunk of one of the riverside alders caught my attention. As I watched, a tiny brownish mouse-like bird proceeded to climb the trunk in a spiral fashion, disappearing from view from time to time, to re-emerge higher still before flying to the base of another tree and repeating the process. Compared with my brief and dramatic encounter with a kingfisher, there could hardly have been a more striking contrast than this first sighting of a treecreeper, one of our least spectacular birds. Yet in some way this new experience made a more lasting impression, reinforcing as it did the quiet pleasure to be had from patiently watching and waiting.

I had by this time acquired an ancient pair of field-glasses, which were to give me years of faithful service until I could afford my first binoculars. Despite their low magnification, these glasses enabled me to observe wild life for the first time in comparative close-up. On one memorable occasion, while mooching along the bank of a small lake, I discovered a tiny ball of woven grasses, hidden in the tangle of branches of an uprooted tree. The neat little entrance hole to what was obviously a nest of some kind was clearly visible from the nearby trunk and I determined to perch myself on this improvised seat and await the arrival - or departure - of its owner.

I was to discover that peering through eyepieces in an uncomfortable position for a length of time can be quite tiring; so much so that it was sorely tempting to give up the vigil and move on. However, I stuck it out and was at last thrilled to see a tiny animal - presumably a field vole - push through the vegetation, inspect the nest, and eventually wriggle inside, causing the fragile structure to bulge and wobble momentarily before resuming its normal shape. Stiff and numb, I clambered down to the ground and went on my way, well rewarded for my patience and discomfort.

*****************

That August saw my third and final youth club seaside holiday. The chosen location was Brighton and Margaret and I made up one of several couples in the party. As always, accommodation arrangements ensured that the sexes were carefully segregated and to my knowledge everyone willingly abided by the unwritten rules. However, the club spirit that had formerly bound us together in one happy family had lost its appeal; disliking the glitter and sophistication of Brighton, we wanted to see something of the Sussex coast and countryside and to achieve this decided to opt out of most of the club activities and instead plan our own holiday.

A choice of bus trips were on offer and on several days we set off for some new destination. The old town of Lewes, in particular, took our fancy and we enjoyed marvellous views westwards from the ramparts of the ruined castle. Steyning and Bramber - again an impressive ruined castle - provided another satisfying day, despite the limited scope for exploring such inviting countryside on foot. In an attempt to discover the supposed delights of the coast for ourselves, we set off one day on foot towards Rottingdean. We were treated to superb cliff-top views - our first of the English Channel - but then, drawn by its alluring name, we made the mistake of boarding a bus for Peacehaven, only to find the coast defiled by a rash of hideous bungalows, which made the return trip to Brighton almost a pleasure by comparison.

******************

Back at work, I was called upon to put in several hours of overtime, assisting Tim Woolley with the laying-out of a new underground district. Although this didn't qualify for extra pay, I was allowed a day's leave in lieu, which I determined to spend cycling in the Peak District. Accordingly, one calm and almost spring-like late September morning, I set off early along the almost deserted roads, bound for the plague village of Eyam. I knew the place well, and had read several accounts of the terrible occurrence of 1665, when a parcel of patterns sent to a journeyman tailor from London brought the dreaded pestilence to this Peakland village, with catastrophic consequences. Eyam was one of those places that drew me back, time and again, and leaving my bike, I spent an absorbing hour or more seeking out yet again the pathetic graves of those who perished during that fateful year.

It was now approaching midday and I decided to press on the five or so miles to Tideswell - another favourite village - where I hoped to buy something to eat before visiting the superb church, justifiably called The Cathedral of the Peak. Seeing a butcher's shop with a display of tempting pork pies in the window, I stopped and went inside. The man behind the counter was talkative; had I heard the news? I'd left home before the morning bulletin, I informed him. Then I wouldn't know that there'd been a bad colliery accident, he told me - and in Derbyshire. I was horrorstruck. Where? I demanded. The man looked confused; after all, Tideswell, high in the Peak, was far removed from the coalfield. He hesitated. Chesterfield way, he thought, but couldn't recall the exact name. Anyway, it sounded bad – men trapped.

I left the shop in a daze. Up to a point, all the pits I had worked at could be described as being Chesterfield way, although many others were much nearer the town. But such idle speculation was futile. At this moment - somewhere in the coalfield where I worked - men were entombed. The horror of three years earlier had returned. Then, in August 1947, less than a year after nationalisation, 104 men had perished in the William Pit at Whitehaven, in Cumberland, shattering the belief that such disasters were nightmares somehow consigned to the past.

Pedalling homeward, the day that had begun with such promise was now irretrievably darkened by the knowledge that sombre news awaited my return. I could summon up no interest in the scenery around me. For once, the miles seemed long and wearisome, the familiar roadside features suddenly remote, irrelevant. There was fear, dismay - and anger too - surging within. To think that people - people I knew - grumbled about the price of coal. This was the *real* price of coal - men's lives. Even now, I could picture groups huddled at the pit-head, silent, numb, awaiting news of loved ones. Wives and mothers, heavy of heart, breaking the news to innocent children, or at best clinging on desperately to forlorn hope, diminishing with every passing, agonising hour.........

I flung open the gate and burst into the kitchen, bracing myself for the news. Father wasted no words. 'Bad fire at Creswell. A lot dead. They're still trying to rescue survivors.'

Creswell Colliery was a large mine between Chesterfield and Mansfield. A fire, caused by a damaged conveyor motor, killed 80 men. 33 bodies were never recovered and had to be sealed in the abandoned workings. For a few days the wider world became aware of the danger men still faced daily in mining coal. Sympathy was expressed and promises made by those in power that steps would be taken to ensure that such a tragedy could never happen again. And then attention was turned to other, more newsworthy events and soon it became acceptable to complain once more about the price of coal.

# Chapter 25

At work, nothing had changed. Nightmare had become ghastly reality not far away at Creswell but at Asherton, as in all the other pits, coal still had to be won and men still had to risk their lives to win it. The disaster was the chief topic of conversation, naturally enough, but sentiment had no place in this world; men talked in muted, matter-of-fact tones. Some could recall a similar loss of life at Markham, not far from Creswell, twelve years earlier, back in the bad old days of private enterprise. At least now there'd be drastic action to prevent a repeat of what went wrong.

And so there was. Rubber conveyor belts were replaced by non-inflammable material and safety precautions were enforced with more vigour than before. One result of this increased emphasis on safety was that the Asherton safety officer was provided with a splendid new office and the survey staff were offered the use of his former lair, which to our relief enabled us to remove our equipment from Larry's telephone exchange and in so doing escape the unwholesome mix of religious fanaticism and sexual frustration that had caused Neville and me such discomfort from the start.

By now I was on good terms with a number of the men I encountered underground. This was especially desirable in the case of the teams of men whose job it was to extend the roadways. As most of my work was concerned with ensuring that these roadways advanced on the correct bearing, a good working relationship was of mutual benefit. Roadway construction - known as ripping in this coalfield - was heavy and dangerous work. Explosive charges were used to blast the rock immediately above the coal seam. The loosened lumps were then brought down by hand pick and laboriously cleared away by shovel. Next, two matching metal arched supports were set in position in the shape of the letter 'n' and bolted together in the roof of the roadway by a pair of brackets. To counter roof falls, timber planks were inserted between each of the arches.

A team of rippers normally consisted of four men, led by an experienced miner. These men took a genuine pride in their work and as well as being generally pleasant and cooperative, were often interesting individuals in their own right. One was an enthusiastic pigeon fancier, with whom I had many a friendly argument over whether the peregrine falcon should be persecuted or protected. Another, a keen fisherman, revealed himself to be something of a naturalist, thanks to his patient vigils by the waterside; while yet another, his own playing days cut short by an injury sustained in the pit, devoted much of his leisure time to running a lads' football team.

As young men rightly considered as having comparatively easy jobs, Neville and I were subjected to a fair amount of good-natured banter. My involvement in amateur dramatics provided plenty of scope for this, while one man's colourfully embellished account of having seen Neville bound purposefully towards a well-known lovers' lane in the company of a pretty girl gave rise to much hilarity. It so happened that the main talking point during the early days of the new year was the daring theft of the Stone of Scone by Scottish nationalists from Westminster Abbey. This had taken place on Christmas Day and its disappearance had the police completely baffled. One morning, as we arrived at one particular roadway extension, the team leader informed me in serious tones that the missing stone had at last been found.

'Oh, and where was this, Harry?' I asked.

'Up the Scotsman's kilt,' was the prompt reply, accompanied by an outburst of laughter from his mates. Well and truly caught out, I uttered a rare obscenity of self-disgust, which sent my hearers into raptures of delight and of which I was constantly reminded whenever we met for months afterwards.

Another group of men with whom good relations were important were the pony gangers. There were about twenty ponies employed at Asherton, housed in well-maintained stables close to the pit bottom - their permanent home except for the fortnight's holiday during the summer. The gangers themselves were young men, gaining experience before promotion to coal-face work and as surveying sometimes necessitated interrupting their routine, it was essential to gain their goodwill.

In overall charge of the gangers and their ponies was a man known as the corporal. He came from a farming background and his prime concern was the wellbeing of the ponies under his care. He had his own little office close by the stables, in which he kept a range of veterinary products and in which any ganger suspected of ill-using his pony was severely dealt with. By now confined exclusively to timber haulage, ponies had formerly been used to haul coal tubs in this and other collieries but the time was long gone when they were cruelly exploited. I was shown a photograph, taken a few years before the first world war, depicting a row of ponies, with their ganger-boy jockeys, about to compete in a 'Pony Derby', organised as part of the pit-holiday entertainment in the days before seaside holidays became affordable for mining folk.

One burly young ganger I encountered from time to time was a free-scoring centre forward in a prominent local team. Such was Eddie's reputation that a scout from a London first division club travelled up to see him play and was so impressed that he was invited to go for a trial. Sadly, he failed to make the grade but never tired of boasting about how he had played alongside famous internationals, readily producing the torn and crumpled invitation, bearing the club's crest and signed by its manager, that had provided him with his all-too-brief experience of the big time.

It was often said in the Derbyshire-Nottinghamshire coalfield that when either county cricket club needed a new fast bowler, all that they had to do was to call down the nearest pit shaft and likely candidates would come running. Like Eddie's near miss at football stardom, Frank - by now middle-aged but still strikingly tall and lithe - had in his prime come close to the fame that would have enabled him to swap his pit clothes permanently for cricket flannels. Even now he generated a fair amount of pace, regularly skittling the opposition for the colliery team. As a fiery-tempered young man, however, he was said to have struck terror into the hearts of even the most accomplished batsmen. County trials followed and Frank's future looked decidedly bright. Until, that is, he had some sort of disagreement with his captain - an amateur with more influence than ability - and was promptly sent packing.

Revenge, when it finally came, was sweet. Back with the colliery team, Frank was selected to play in a charity match for a representative eleven against the county side, captained by the toff who had earlier caused his downfall. Needless to say, charity was the last thing on Frank's mind as he hurled down a succession of unplayable deliveries to tear the heart out of the county's batting, bowling the captain neck-and-crop in the process. Frank was now a maintenance man, his huge hands making light work of lifting heavy conveyor pans and his powerful shoulders seeming to respond effortlessly as he hauled great rolls of belt into position. On one occasion, I overheard him admonish the youth assisting him and the air was blue with expletive. It occurred to me that if he had turned on anything like such a flow of vocabulary all those years ago, it was little wonder that his career as a county cricketer ended before it had even begun.

That spring, my own undistinguished cricketing career staged a brief revival. The area survey staff had expanded to such a degree that it became possible to field an eleven to play a handful of evening matches against other departments. Having by now ceased to emulate my former hero, Keith Miller, I applied myself to cautious batting and slow line-and-length bowling of the kind that my former superior, Mr Elliston, had advocated, and gained some modest success at both. The peak of my achievement was to hang on grimly and play out a maiden over in virtual darkness against a wily spin bowler and so save a game against superior opposition, spurred on in the knowledge that Margaret was among the handful of spectators somewhere in the distant gloom.

# Chapter 26

**O**ccasionally - very occasionally - the monotony of life underground was enlivened by the impinging of some minor event on the daily routine. It so happened that extensive opencast mining operations were taking place in the area around the village and the excavators exposed the workings of an ancient coal mine not far from my home. This discovery was brought to the attention of the local historian whose evening classes I attended during the winter months and he carried out a detailed inspection of the site. His findings - tools, candles, clay pipes and other miscellaneous items - were listed in an article he wrote for the county archaeological society's journal and reading it renewed my interest in the history of mining, confirming as it did that digging for coal had been going on in these parts since medieval times.

So when, a short time later, a new development at Asherton made contact with the abandoned workings of an earlier colliery, I was quickly on the scene, determined to see for myself any vestiges of the old mine that had come to light. However, I was in for a disappointment. For a start, the workings had been abandoned as recently as the 1920s and most of the evidence - old newspapers - bore unmistakable signs of the use to which they had been put. But at least I had the satisfaction of seeing how well the timber supports had withstood 30 years of entombment and could read the chalked messages - still as clear as on the day they were written by the long-departed miners.

It was at about this time that a serious geological problem occurred in another part of the mine. Faults - fractures in the strata caused by massive earth movements - were a common feature in the coalfield and although most were comparatively small and didn't unduly interfere with production, hitting a large fault caused a major disruption, often necessitating the workings to dip or climb to regain the seam. This particular fault, although encountered in neighbouring mines, proved to be far larger than anticipated. A dramatic upheaval must have taken place at some stage in the geological past, causing the seam to disappear from view, in this case downwards. Suddenly there was no coal.

BRJ was informed and accompanied by his two under-managers, he strode off to inspect the scene. Along with others not directly involved, I tactfully withdrew, though not before my ears had been assailed by some of the manager's choicest invective, the thunderous tones of which carried throughout the nearby workings. Large faults such as this one presented a difficult dilemma for a colliery manager. For not only did the temporary loss of the seam halt coal extraction but the only way to regain the seam was to drive tunnels, known as headings, through solid rock. These headings had to be graded in such a way that the conveyors and haulage tracks could operate efficiently and this was both slow and expensive work.

The danger element added to the complications. The layers of strata displaced by a fault were often extremely unstable and the risk of roof falls was a constant source of concern. To minimise this risk, extra roof supports were set in faulty ground but these were soon crushed and buckled by the pressure from above and had to be regularly renewed. The exposure of so much overlying strata revealed an exceptional range of fossils, especially giant tree ferns, and as an avid collector, I was sorely tempted to try to extract some of these. It took one sudden shower of rock fragments to deter me, however, and from then on I had to be content with admiring them by the light of my lamp.

Naturally enough, the fault became the chief talking point throughout the pit and gave rise to many tales of happenings connected with previous encounters with these geological phenomena. I was told of one miner, long since dead, who, like many of his contemporaries, was in the habit of sucking a small cobble of coal as he worked. According to the story, a large fault was struck and a heading was driven to regain the seam. However, when the man tasted the coal, he declared it to be from a different seam from the one they had been working. His mates ridiculed him at first but soon afterwards they struck another fault and tests proved beyond doubt that owing to the complex nature of that particular area, the seams had been subjected to so much pressure that the one being worked had been lost and they had instead made contact with another.

Even in parts of the mine free from faulting, the coal seams seldom lay horizontally at Asherton, for like the other pits at which I worked, it lay on the rim of the coalfield and the strata had been subjected to considerable disturbance in distant geological time. It followed that gradients of varying steepness were a common occurrence throughout the mine and it was while working on one of these inclines that I made an error of judgment that could well have had disastrous consequences.

Assisted by Neville, I was about to extend the line in a gently-climbing roadway leading to one of the more remote coal faces. To my annoyance, however, I found that the sight-line was obscured by a single pit tub, loaded with a section of a coal-cutting machine awaiting removal for repair, which stood unattended on the rails near the brow of the incline. As there was no sign of the fitters responsible for removing this obstruction, I decided that we could do it ourselves; all that was required was to gently lower the tub a distance of about twenty  yards, using the wooden pegs, known as lockers, which were inserted between the spokes to act as a brake.

What I had failed to allow for was that while removing lockers from stationary wheels was easy enough, inserting them into turning wheels was a different matter entirely. In short, the moment we extracted the lockers, the heavily-loaded tub began to move and despite our frantic efforts to replace them, the runaway soon picked up speed and careered out of control into the darkness. Numb with dismay, we followed the eerie rumble. Fervently I prayed that no-one was approaching up the incline. For although refuge holes had been left in the sides of the roadway at intervals, the tub was travelling at such a speed by now that anyone hearing it bearing down on them would need to take rapid evasive action. And what if a pony was on the way up? Sick with apprehension, we stumbled on.

Suddenly, there was a tremendous crash, followed by silence. Even now it is with a shudder that I recall the agonising suspense - a minute or two at most, but it seemed an age - as we neared the scene. What we found in the cloud of settling dust was the derailed tub on its end amidst a tangle of broken rails, and the section of the cutting machine lying several yards away. The thankfulness I experienced that no-one had been killed was - and is still - impossible to explain. I seem to remember fighting back the tears of relief that mingled with bursts of uncontrollable laughter. When at last our composure was more or less restored, we set off to report what had happened to the district deputy, bracing ourselves for the reprimand that I, at least, fully deserved.

Yet again, we were fortunate. The official in charge that day was a cheerful, friendly man whom I knew quite well and whose plans for the erection of a garage I had drawn recently for an absurdly cheap fee. Even so, it was with more than a little trepidation that we accompanied him to the crash scene and waited in subdued silence as he inspected the results of my folly. It could, he conceded, have been worse-much worse. No-one was injured and as the cutter section was to be replaced anyway, the damage was minimal. The rails would have to be re-laid, of course, and that meant expense. That would have to go in his report book - standard procedure.

Neville blurted out the question that I too, was burning to ask. 'Will Mr Jefferson find out?'

The deputy gave a low chuckle. 'What the eye doesna' see, the 'eart doesna' grieve.'

We gulped our thanks. I had learned a bitter lesson.

# Chapter 27

**D**espite having successfully completed my journalism course, my writing career had yet to advance beyond the raw beginner stage. True, my nature notes were still appearing regularly in the local weekly paper, and still bringing in a penny-halfpenny a line. And I was steadily amassing a cuttings library, reading widely, and adding to my library of books, as much as my limited funds would allow. But the way ahead seemed far from clear; I had an uneasy feeling that I lacked a sense of purpose yet seemed unable to get to grips with the problem.

I was by now approaching my twenty-first birthday and was still handing over my wages to Mother and receiving pocket money in return. It was with some reluctance that my parents at last agreed that on reaching my maturity, I could begin paying for my board - something my contemporaries had been doing for some time. Mrs Fairbrother, meanwhile, was growing impatient at my lack of progress as a writer. Father had mentioned my forthcoming birthday and she had seized the opportunity to apply some pressure on my behalf.

'I told him that you'll never be taken seriously as a writer without a typewriter,' she announced when we met in the street one day. 'I explained to him that the money he spent on your course might just as well have been thrown away if he doesn't provide the means for you to sell your work.' A grim little smile of triumph spread over the pugnacious, thrusting face. 'It was hard work but I got him to see sense in the end. I told him that he can get hold of a reconditioned typewriter without breaking the bank.' She caught my eye and held it challengingly. 'Then you can get down to some serious writing - and not before time.'

Sure enough, Father had been spurred into action. Knowing how Mother would react if he revealed the origins of his deliberations, he trod warily.

'I've been reading about these new-fangled portable typewriters,' he said casually. 'Strikes me that he needs one for his writing.' He produced the newspaper advertisement. 'And they're noiseless as well, according to this.'

Mother detected a snag. 'But he can't type - and we can't help him.' I was tempted to suggest that I ask Margaret, an experienced typist, to give me lessons but as she hadn't yet been asked to tea, and bearing in mind my unfortunate experience with Mother and Rita, I thought better of it.

Father's mind was made up, however. 'He can learn, like anybody else. Once he's got it, it's up to him.' I mentioned reconditioned machines. Again, Father was adamant.

'It'll be a new one - or none at all,' he declared emphatically 'You're only twenty-one once.'

\*\*\*\*\*\*\*\*\*\*\*\*\*\*\*\*\*

Sundays were Peak District days. Undeterred by our first rain-swept bike ride, Margaret and I set off early for the hills and dales, determined to make the most of our precious leisure hours in seeking out new routes, exploring villages, visiting churches, watching wild life and compiling, with our cheap little cameras, a motley collection of black and white photographs of sights and scenes that took our fancy.

Cromford - some ten miles distant - was more often than not our immediate destination. From this crossroads village on the River Derwent, any number of exciting possibilities beckoned. To the north, beyond the rocky portal of Scarthin Nick, lay the Matlocks - tripper attractions recalled with delight from childhood, with the snaking gorge of Derwent Dale surmounted by the awe-inspiring landmarks of High Tor and the Heights of Abraham. Beyond still lay the glory of the White Peak; roughly-hewn villages of sun-glinting limestone that seemed to have sprung from the very rock itself - Winster, Youlgreave, Over Haddon, Monyash - places that drew us time and time again, just to linger in and soak up the atmosphere. Often we would leave our bikes and wander by clear, fast-flowing streams, scale sparsely-grassed ridges or merely sit on a flower-spangled bank with birds and butterflies for company.

On other occasions we headed north-west from Cromford along the winding, wooded Via Gellia, before climbing steadily through wide stone-wall country towards Hartington and the Staffordshire border. Here, the lovely River Dove threaded its delicate way southwards, heading for incomparable Dovedale. Later, the dale itself yielded up its treasures to us; it meant pushing our bikes the nine miles along the riverside, followed by a long ride home from Thorpe Cloud, but the rewards were beyond price. This was the Derbyshire of the books I was gradually acquiring, with their alluring sepia tone photographs - the land praised by poets and sought out by discerning pilgrims from afar. And now, with a likeminded companion, every spring and summer Sunday, it was mine to enjoy too.

In sharp contrast to the limestone landscape of the White Peak was the gritstone country to the east. Beyond the dark weather-beaten stone villages of Milltown and Ashover stretched mile upon mile of open moorland, extending in a massive sweep from above Chatsworth's sumptuous parkland and beyond the sprawl of Chesterfield into Yorkshire. Up here, vast rocky outcrops reared stark away on distant horizons, while the heather carpet changed in hue with the interplay of sunshine and cloud above.

Having parted company with the youth club, and with our annual holidays drawing near, we found ourselves in something of a dilemma. We were by now regular visitors to one another's homes and inevitably the subject was discussed in some detail, though inconclusively, with both sets of parents. We had made it clear that we wanted to spend the holiday together but how could this be arranged without the involvement of some organisation, such as the youth club, to ensure that propriety was observed? At last I had an idea. Mother's younger brother had a small farm in Leicestershire. Could we take our bikes and spend a week there? To my pleasant surprise, this was agreed to. Letters were exchanged - we had no telephone - and everything was arranged. Our bikes could be sent on ahead by train and we would follow by bus. In the meantime, equipped with our indispensable Bartholomew half-inch maps, we got down to planning the routes we intended to follow on our daily rides, while at the same time making full use of the Leicestershire volume of Arthur Mee's *King's England* series of county guides to ensure that we included as many attractive-sounding villages in our itineraries as we possibly could.

We were given the warmest of welcomes. For years, my hard-working, yet perpetually cheerful uncle and his generous-natured wife had tried in vain to persuade my parents to return the yearly flying visits they paid to us. Now, for the first time in my life, I could enjoy a country holiday, explore a landscape new to me in the company of my girl friend, and return each evening to generous helpings of farmhouse fare and an audience eager to hear a detailed account of the day's exploits.

Compared with the Peak District, the Leicestershire countryside could hardly have been less spectacular. But to us, pedalling along deserted country lanes, armed with our notes on what to see culled from Arthur Mee and our map for ever at the ready, this was nothing less than a journey of discovery. Every church along the way was assiduously sought out, visited and photographed; no imposing manor house was missed; no engaging group of thatched cottages passed without an admiring glance.

We had reserved our last day for our most ambitious ride, a 50-mile round trip that would take us over the county boundary into England's smallest county, Rutland. I had long cherished this ambition and on the return journey, triumphant at having fulfilled it at last, we resolved that on our future holidays, we would explore all the English counties one by one, beginning with Rutland, and that I would write a book on each; or if not an actual book, then at least an informative article for publication in a top-quality magazine. This, I reasoned, would establish my reputation as a serious writer; no squalid, nose-to- the-ground newshound scribbling for me. Instead, I would devote my life to travelling - by bike and on foot - exploring the countryside and delighting an eager readership with a new offering at regular intervals.

But first, I must have the essential tool of my trade - a typewriter. And with my twenty-first birthday approaching, I hadn't long to wait.

# Chapter 28

I sailed into 1952 on the crest of a wave. I was now paying for my weekly board, which left me five pounds to spend or save as I wished. I was the proud possessor of a brand new typewriter. And I had been given a leading role in the opening play of the new year. By happy chance, my twenty-first birthday occurred during the play's four-night run and I basked in the attention - and especially in the unscripted hugs and kisses bestowed by the female members of the cast.

Post-production euphoria had scarcely died down when an event in the greater world jolted us all back to reality. News of the untimely death of the king was received at the colliery with genuine dismay. Miners weren't generally considered to be among the more enthusiastic upholders of the monarchy but during his fifteen years' reign, George V1 had won the respect and affection of his subjects and his loss was keenly felt. So much so that the attempt by one official to joke about the event fell upon stony silence.

On the day of the funeral, the colliery hooter announced the official silence, and it was a moving experience to stand bareheaded in the pit yard, alongside Mr Jefferson and men from all departments, recalling the train of tumultuous events through which this gentle king had been our figurehead, and who would now be succeeded by the first queen for over half a century.

\*\*\*\*\*\*\*\*\*\*\*\*\*\*\*\*\*

As Mrs Fairbrother was quick to remind me, I, now had a typewriter and the sooner I became proficient in its use, the better. Never one to master unfamiliar operations easily, my first attempts at producing acceptable typescript were, to say the least, discouraging. I had no alternative but to press on, however, and gradually some semblance of what I deemed adequate began to emerge, albeit after what seemed like hours of one-finger concentration. Eventually I judged that the time had come for me to attempt to break into print, or at least to extend my range beyond my weekly scribblings for the local paper.

It so happened that the evening paper had recently reported a speech given by a local MP - a government minister who was also a prominent lawyer, a profession which Father held in special contempt. The gist of the speech, as far as I could understand it, was that the miners' achievements in raising record amounts of coal since nationalisation should be recognised as selfless sacrifice on behalf of the nation, worthy of unqualified praise. Listening to Father's scornful reaction to what he called this twaddle, and still woefully ignorant of political matters, I composed a letter intended to put across Father's views while at the same time identifying with the miners. This clumsy, ill-judged attempt to bridge a political chasm was promptly printed on the correspondence page, complete with my name and address.

Mother was horrified. Sweeping aside Father's assurances that my letter - if read at all - would be instantly forgotten, she launched into a tirade against politicians, miners, newspaper editors - but most of all against me.

'Why can't you just be normal?' she wailed. 'Why do you have to be different - all this writing and getting mixed up in politics and the Lord knows what. I just can't understand you - all these big ideas'. In exasperation, she shifted her attack to the woman she saw as the arch-villain of the piece. 'Lady Muck - that's whose to blame for all this!' she raged. 'Sticking her nose into other folks' affairs. And you're happy to let her - both of you!'

For once, Father and I were joint objects of her wrath, enduring her taunts together, subdued and silent.

Whatever consequences Mother may have feared would result from my impulsive entry into the world of newspaper debate, she needn't have worried. No bricks were hurled through our windows and no slogans were daubed on our door. In short, if anyone in the village read the letter, they chose not to broach the subject. One of the miners' union officials enquired casually whether I was the writer and on hearing my confession made some non-committal remark; otherwise the matter sank without trace. However, I had learned yet another lesson - the world of politics was not for me. Instead, I would concentrate on subjects I knew something about - and hopefully earn some money in the process.

My next step along the road to literary fame was a cautious one. I approached the editor of the county weekly paper, suggesting a regular column on country matters. To my pleasant surprise this was promptly agreed to at a fee of fifteen shillings (75p) for a 300-word piece. Elated, I informed the local paper that I would no longer be submitting work to them and turned my attention to assembling sufficient subject matter to ensure that I would be able to fill my column for several weeks to come.

Meanwhile, my after-work bike rides were directed increasingly towards the study of birds. Following memorable encounters with the kingfisher and treecreeper, I was beginning to learn that patient observation brought rich rewards. And so, during that spring, armed with my ancient field glasses, what proved to be a lifelong source of pleasure began to unfold. I discovered that birds I had assumed would shun the heavily industrialised environment in which I lived were in fact present, and that, after a day spent underground, watching them going about their lives was an immensely enjoyable and satisfying experience. Seldom did a ride fail to produce a new bird - bullfinch, reed bunting, long-tailed tit, willow warbler, whitethroat – all were identified and triumphantly recorded in the pages of my nature diary.

Membership of the Royal Society for the Protection of Birds enhanced this pleasure, as did founder-membership of the Derbyshire Ornithological Society, at a meeting of which a lecture on the feeding habits of owls made an immediate impact. As a result of this, I embarked on a painstaking search for the regurgitated pellets of our local pair of little owls and in so doing learned of their partiality for beetles, mice, voles and the occasional starling; one pellet I discovered contained wing feathers from the luckless victim. However, this increasing involvement in bird watching exposed the severe limitations of my field glasses and I began to set aside a small amount each month towards the purchase of a pair of binoculars, a bewildering range of which were by now available, though at prices well beyond my means.

An even more pressing priority at this time concerned our summer holiday. Recalling with pleasure our week in Leicestershire, and in particular our ride into Rutland, Margaret and I determined to spend our precious holiday week exploring England's smallest county, which, I fondly imagined, would pave the way to the first of my books on the counties of England. To begin with, however, we had to persuade our parents to agree to something entirely beyond their experience - an unmarried couple holidaying together, alone. When at last, following the giving of solemn assurances, consent was granted, there remained the matter of obtaining suitable accommodation. This I at length achieved by combing the holiday columns of newspapers and in time we found ourselves installed - in separate rooms - in a delightful cottage in a village close to the little town of Uppingham. Our hostess was a vigilant-eyed widow who in term-time accommodated boys from the nearby public school, and who, on the slightest pretext, entered my room without warning, assuring me that, familiar as she was with the ways of the youthful male, nothing whatever could possibly surprise her.

Rutland enchanted us. As on our Leicestershire holiday, we mapped out daily rides to incorporate as many villages as possible, made copious notes, snapped every church, manor house and picturesque cottage we could find, and revelled in the freedom, fresh air and daintily-prepared evening meals set before us by our hostess, who proved to be an excellent cook.

It was not until I returned home and had time to assess the jumbled notes I had scribbled on our various rides that the realisation of the immensity of the task I had set myself finally dawned. The plain truth was that I hadn't the faintest idea how to go about writing a book - on Rutland, or on any other subject, come to that. All was not lost, however; I had come across a little magazine published by the Cooperative Society containing short illustrated articles on a range of subjects, including the countryside. Although a book on Rutland was clearly beyond my powers, surely a short article was possible? I did a word-count of features in the current edition, wrote what I hoped was a piece of comparable style, enclosed the best of the photographs we had taken - and waited.

After what seemed an age, the photograph was returned, together with a brief letter accepting the article. There followed another and much longer wait before *England's Smallest County* finally appeared, as eventually did a cheque for two guineas. At last, I felt justified in considering myself a published writer.

# Chapter 29

Modest success with my writing, though gratifying in itself, seemed to further emphasise the dead-end nature of my daily work. Immersed by now in local history and ornithology, and with my mind teeming with ideas for articles on a range of subjects, increasing frustration and bitterness began to disturb the hitherto fairly placid tempo of life. I began to see my work as a prison sentence, with no remission possible, and with my twenty-sixth birthday release as an almost unattainable goal on the distant horizon. The alternative was to wish time- and my youth – away; an equally depressing prospect.

Relationships at work made the situation worse. I continued to get on well enough with the men I encountered on my daily rounds underground; the difficulties arose through changes on the survey staff. For although Tim Woolley, my immediate superior, remained affable enough, he was accompanied on his visits by a succession of youthful assistants, more often than not younger than myself, a few of whom clearly regarded linesmen as inferior mortals, to be treated with contempt. One of these was an especially arrogant character, who on hearing from Tim that I had formerly worked on the staff and aspired to a career outside mining, went out of his way to humiliate me at every opportunity.

Enduring the daily monotony of my job was made no easier by the temperament of Neville, my assistant. He lived some distance from the colliery and like me, cycled to work. Unfortunately he was a reluctant riser, especially after a late night out with his girl friend, and often arrived at the pit-head baths changing room minutes before we were due to descend. This meant that he had a frantic rush to collect his lamp and equipment and join me at the pit top, thus leaving no time to discuss the day's work, let alone exchange pleasantries. Not that pleasantries featured much in our relationship; for Neville, unlike Derek, my perpetually cheerful assistant at Hallfield, was an introverted character, quick to take offence and given to brooding silences which at their worst persisted throughout the entire shift.

During prolonged spells of severe wintry weather, when I was forced to travel to work by bus, Neville, who lived off a bus route, sometimes failed to show up at all. I was given no warning of these absences and had no alternative but to cope single-handedly as best I could. Inevitably, this disrupted the normal work pattern, to the extent that on Neville's return we often had to work a longer-than-usual shift to catch up on the backlog.

One winter's day, having done what I could alone and feeling a little off-colour, I surfaced earlier than usual with the intention of telephoning Tim Woolley and reporting sick. Emerging through the ventilation doors into the open air, I discovered a landscape under snow. Apart from the great chimney, the entire colliery had been covered, as though by magic, in a Christmas-card blanket, its starkness softened and its disfigurements obliterated. Even the giant spoil heap, normally grey and forbidding, resembled some snow-capped peak, presiding over a world untouched by human defilement. And like a blanket, the snowfall had replaced the rawness of the early morning with cheering warmth which, because of its transitoriness, seemed to beckon me to savour its delights there and then.

And so, still in my pit dirt, I set off across the colliery yard, past the cluster of houses and along the field path, my boot prints the first to mark the virgin snow. I had followed this path on a few occasions previously, for it led past a tract of marshy ground and over a footbridge spanning a brook to reach a minor road off the main highway to Chesterfield.

Never before, however, had it revealed its hidden beauty as now, when, like a schoolboy playing truant for the first time, I revelled in the stolen experience, lingering beneath the waterside alders, oblivious to the demands of the workaday world.

\*\*\*\*\*\*\*\*\*\*\*\*\*\*\*\*\*

Occasionally the humdrum daily routine was enlivened by some occurrence which, though trivial in itself, served to relieve the monotony and in time acquired a quality verging almost on folklore. With the survey department, in common with other branches of the industry, continually expanding, a steady flow of young trainees came and went, gaining experience at different collieries under the direction of unit surveyors. One such recruit - a gangling former grammar schoolboy of cultured speech and impeccable manners - was placed for a time with Tim Woolley and received his first taste of pit work at Asherton. His refined ways provoked a good deal of ridicule during the shift but this was as nothing compared with the commotion that erupted when we stripped off in the pithead showers. For the lad proved to be endowed with an appendage of such phenomenal size that his tormentors could only exclaim in mingled amazement and envy at what they saw.

Word of this awe-inspiring sight quickly spread and the poor youth could only cringe in embarrassment as the entire workforce, or so it seemed, contrived to shower at the same time, craning their necks for a better view of this remarkable piece of anatomy. The culmination of this episode occurred one Sunday afternoon. Tim Woolley and his expanded team, including the well-endowed youth, Neville and myself, had completed a special survey and draped in towels, were making our way from the showers towards the clean lockers when I heard suppressed giggles in the otherwise empty baths.

Suddenly, without warning, Tim and his deputy – he who regarded the right to humiliate subordinates as a perk of his position – seized the unsuspecting trainee, pulled away his towel, and after pinning his arms behind his back, frogmarched him into the main corridor, where two young women were waiting. To his credit, the lad writhed and kicked with such ferocity that the voyeurs' pleasure was short-lived and they fled in hysterical disorder.

The young trainee moved on shortly after this incident, though whether he stayed the course in the hard world of mining I never did find out. And although his remarkable physical characteristic remained a topic of conversation long afterwards, the nature of his humiliation that afternoon was seldom if ever referred to.

*****************

Although by now I knew several of the Asherton miners quite well, some of whom lived close to my own home, only seldom did I encounter a familiar face away from the pit itself. For unlike the  Hallfield men, many of whom were true countrymen – smallholders, gardeners, poachers even – my present workmates seemed to have little affinity with the countryside, even though comparatively unspoilt stretches of it were within easy reach.  I was told of gambling rings taking place along the footpath I had walked in the snow and dark rumours circulated from time to time of clandestine cockfights in a derelict farm building nearby. But apart from exchanging greetings with the occasional dog walker, I had the local footpaths to myself.

Until that is, on one of my late afternoon visits to a stretch of the local river, close to where I had caught my first and only glimpse of a kingfisher. On this particular occasion, the footbridge on which I normally lingered was draped with a motley assortment of clothing, the owners of which – two men and several young children – were thoroughly absorbed some distance away downstream, fishing, paddling, climbing trees and obviously enjoying themselves. Just as I was about to move on, I was greeted by a familiar voice, that of a young coal-face worker whose changing locker was close to my own and with whom I had often exchanged idle banter. I walked along the bank to the scene of the fun and the miner, and what proved to be his elder brother, emerged from the water, as surprised to see me as I was to see them. I learned that both families lived in cottages on the edge of a nearby colliery village; they had worked in the pit since leaving school but had retained their love of the countryside and saw sharing this with their children as the natural way of life. Conversation turned to birds and it soon became clear that the brothers possessed a sound practical knowledge of the subject. I was surprised to hear the vernacular names for common birds - scribble lark for the yellowhammer, jenny for the wren, peggy for the whitethroat and spink for the chaffinch – still used, having wrongly assumed that they had been consigned to the realm of folk-lore. The brothers too had seen a kingfisher on this stretch of the river and one of them gave a clear description of the grey wagtail - a bird unknown to me at the time but which I recorded nearby soon afterwards. And although I never again encountered this happy little group on my wanderings, from then on my encounters with either brother, in the baths or below ground, were always pleasant occasions, as I learned of their latest adventures by the river and in the nearby fields and woods.

# Chapter 30

Freelance writing, I soon discovered, was a hazardous occupation. Every modest achievement seemed to be counterbalanced by a disappointment and although my typing was gradually improving, my random attempts to break into fresh markets were rewarded with an ever-increasing number of rejection slips.

Even my initial success with the Cooperative Society magazine proved to be beginner's luck. Rashly assuming that the editor would be eager to accept more articles on countryside topics, I hastily dispatched others, only to be thanked for my submissions but informed that on this occasion the editor regrets, etc., etc.

Father, unfamiliar with the ways of editors, smelt a rat. Some years earlier, he had exchanged heated words with a prominent local Society official and was convinced that this man - by now a Labour councillor and in the process of effectively distancing himself from his working-class origins - had read my article and had taken steps to ensure that my literary career, in the Society's magazine at least, should be stopped in its tracks.

Mother, predictably, donned her I-told-you-so mantle. Recalling my ill-judged venture into newspaper correspondence-column politics, she saw this latest threat to her nervous state as a direct result of the publication of my name in the first place.

'As if I haven't got enough to bother about,' she lamented. 'Worries me sick, it does. All this –.' Unable to find words to express her exasperation, her protests petered out in despair.

Not all my feverish attempts to sell my work ended in failure, however. Devouring the cricket scores in the *Manchester Guardian* one evening, I noticed that Eric

Hollies, the Warwickshire spin bowler, whose ineptitude with the bat assured him of the permanent number eleven place in his county's batting order, had excelled himself by accumulating what was for him a record-breaking score of 30-odd runs on the previous day. As a diligent student of cricket statistics, this led me to ponder the phenomenon of bowlers notoriously weak as batsmen, a subject, I reasoned, that might appeal to the paper's daily *Miscellany* column.

By the time I had roughed out a short piece on the subject it was well past bedtime and the effort of concentration after a day spent underground was beginning to tell. I knew, however, that unless I posted it next morning, my article would have lost its topicality so there was no alternative but to polish it up and type it before I went to bed.

There followed an exhausting hour or more in which, after striving my utmost to emulate the newspaper's style, I set about typing the piece to what I imagined would be an acceptable standard. It was at this stage that fatigue combined with anxiety to confound my intentions; erratic spacing, variable margins, indifferent spelling and punctuation - all shortcomings that in normal circumstances would not have arisen - defied my efforts time and again.

At last, weary and dispirited, I sealed the far-from-perfect final attempt in its envelope ready to post on my way to work the following morning, determined to forget the entire episode. But that was easier said than done. Arriving home a few days later, I opened the paper warily and heart racing in anticipation, turned to the page on which *Miscellany* appeared. And there - under the heading The Worst Batsman?– was my article, word for word as I had written it, though in keeping with all the other contributions, printed anonymously.

Payment – fourteen shillings and sixpence – arrived some time later. The amount was, as Father put it 'Better than a kick in the teeth - though not much,' but at least I felt a renewed surge of confidence, for although I posed no threat as yet to the likes of Neville Cardus, at least I'd been published in the *Manchester Guardian*.

*****************

It was to be the countryside, and birds in particular, rather than cricket, that provided me with the breakthrough I sought. For as well as our walks and cycle rides, I was by now reading widely on several aspects of country life and my short weekly newspaper pieces no longer offered sufficient scope for the kind of writing I wanted to produce.

Accordingly, I submitted a lengthy article on the wildlife of a local derelict canal to the *Derbyshire Countryside* magazine, which the editor promptly accepted and published, lavishly illustrated by a prominent local photographer. I followed this up with a light-hearted piece describing how I had risen early on a wet spring morning to hear the dawn chorus and another tracing the arrival in and successful colonisation of the county by the alien little owl. In each case the editor took the trouble to write a courteous and friendly letter of acceptance. I was overjoyed. My parents meanwhile, untroubled by fears of recrimination or suspicion, were able at last to share in my satisfaction.

My article on the little owl had been illustrated by one of the county's most prominent ornithologists and the chairman of the newly-formed society of which I was a member. I held the great man in awe and had always been tongue-tied in his presence; now, however, as a result of the article, all this was about to change. Margaret and I had booked places on the society's bird-watching weekend in Norfolk and during the course of a memorable few days we became acquainted not only with the chairman but also with a number of other ornithologists from all walks of life. To our pleasant surprise, we discovered that the sharing of a common interest swept away any trace of the social barriers we had imagined existed and we were readily accepted by our fellow members. By this time we were both equipped with binoculars and first-ever sightings of marsh harriers, short-eared owls and bearded tits, among others, ensured that the Norfolk coast would command a place in our affections for years to come.

By now, birds had become supremely important in my life and the pleasure they gave me defies mere words to describe. And while the sighting of a rarity brought satisfaction in the extreme, I never tired of watching familiar species which - now my powers of observation were sharpened - seemed to occur in totally unexpected places. Pied wagtails, for instance, seemed attracted to the colliery spoil heap, and would often flit busily over the still - smouldering rubble along the tip margins. Starlings and house sparrows found congenial nesting conditions amid the high roofs of the pit-head buildings; and I was taken to see the nest of a trusting pair of blackbirds, built on a beam in one of the workshops, where they were treated like honoured guests by the men working below.

That spring, when my work underground went smoothly and I was able to surface earlier than usual, I formed the habit of slipping off - still in my pit clothes - down the nearby fields to a tract of marshy ground by the brook, along which I had once glimpsed a speeding kingfisher. One afternoon, convinced that this patch of wetland must surely attract something out of the ordinary, I put to flight a greyish- brown wading bird with prominent white hind wings, which uttered a loud repetitive cry as it circled the marsh before landing some distance away, where it merged instantly with its surroundings. Before my weekend in

Norfolk, this bird had been unknown to me; now I had the satisfaction of recording my first- ever redshank close to home.

On another occasion, when my attention was attracted by a party of tree sparrows in a clump of hollowed-out willows, I determined to wait patiently to familiarise myself with a bird I had never before viewed at close quarters. Without binoculars, this proved to be a lengthy exercise and by the time I set off back towards the colliery it was well past my end-of-shift time.

Usually, the only men I encountered along the footpath were a few early-shift miners taking a short cut down to the bus stop on the valley road. On this occasion, however, a familiar thick-set figure suddenly loomed ahead, striding purposefully in my direction, our converging steps destined to meet long before I could possibly take evading action behind the nearest clump of bushes.

Although no sign of recognition revealed itself on the manager's face as we drew level, I had already decided on my course of action.

'Good afternoon, Mr Jefferson,' I volunteered, with what I hoped passed for a mixture of respect, self-confidence and pleasant surprise; after all, he wasn't my direct superior, but if he reported me to the chief surveyor… . Our eyes met. What I took to be an initial twinkle was reassuring, the frown that replaced it less so.

'Hmm. What are you doing, lad?' came the growl.

There was no going back now. 'Bird watching, sir.' I answered as calmly as I could. 'Finished my work early today. Thought I'd take a look at the marsh before my shower – seemed a likely spot.'

My explanation was received with a grunt, followed by a hollow laugh. 'Bird watching, eh?' He swept on.

The following afternoon, as I passed the telephone office

on my way home, Larry tapped on his window. 'Mr Jefferson wants to see you,' he announced importantly as I entered. 'Don't know what for – he didn't say.'

I knocked and braced myself, awaiting the growled response. The manager looked up from his desk and reached for a book. 'Here – borrow this. It'll help with your bird watching - it did with mine, anyway.'

I gulped my thanks, sidestepped Larry's attempted interception, and cycled home, the precious volume tucked safely in my bike bag. *British Birds in their Haunts*, I read. And then, opening the book, my eyes fell on the inscription: 'Awarded to B.R. Jefferson. Lower Forms Nature Prize. Sedbergh School. 1917.'

# Chapter 31

Two books - somewhat worse for wear now but still among my treasured possessions - played an influential part in my life during the early 1950s. The first of these was *Rambling in Derbyshire*, by Jack Helyer, better known as the organist who rose into view from the hidden depths of a Nottingham cinema. With its sepia-tone cover and matching illustrations, as well as small cluttered sketch maps and densely-packed text, it looks distinctly unappealing to the modern rambler. But for Margaret and me it opened up a whole new world – the countryside as revealed from the public footpath.

Hitherto, our explorations had been confined to surfaced roads suitable for cycling and walking, the only exceptions being Dovedale, through which we had pushed our bikes; canal towpaths; and a few familiar field path walks close to home. But now, thanks to this pocket-size three shillings-and-sixpenny book, we had a choice of eighteen tempting rambles, all from bus routes, covering not only the Peak District but the entirely unknown Trent valley, in the south of the county as well.

From now on, our precious weekends were divided between cycling and walking; however, the latter activity, with its unlimited scope for bird-watching along the way, gradually emerged as the preferred option. And although Helyer's routes generally proved straightforward enough to follow, the logical next step was to buy our own Ordnance Survey maps – One Inch to begin with, with the wonderfully detailed Two and a Half Inch later – and begin planning our own walks. Thanks to Helyer's book, we already possessed a basic knowledge of map-reading and this proved invaluable as we embarked on the absorbing activity of matching the features of the landscape before us with those marked on the map in our hands.

Not that all these early self-planned rambles went according to plan. What with way-marking often sparse and in places non-existent, and rights-of-way - on the One Inch maps at least - almost too faintly drawn to follow, getting lost was an occupational hazard. Sometimes we ended up miles out of our way before realising our error; at times like this, fearful of missing the one and only bus home, what began as a leisurely walk ended up as a frantic race against the clock.

As our map-reading skills grew, so too did our confidence. We began buying maps covering other scenically appealing areas – the Cotswolds, Exmoor, the Welsh Marches – which we hoped to visit and explore during the course of future annual holidays. At the rate of two weeks a year, these would take us well into the future, by which time I would have exchanged the life of colliery linesman for successful author.

It was at about this time that, while browsing along the shelves in a second-hand bookshop, I came across the second of the two books that was to play a significant part in my life. Shorn of its dust jacket, its green spine badly faded, it caught my attention solely because the name of the river in its title – Windrush – struck me as one of the most beautiful words I had ever heard. And still does.

Opening the book, I discovered that *The River Windrush*, published in 1946, was an account of a journey made by the author, Wilson Macarthur, and his wife, on foot along the 30-odd miles of a Cotswold river from its source to its meeting with the Thames. No thrill-a-page exotic adventure, in other words, but a chattily informative day-by-day journal – the work of a man whose obvious delight in discovering the commonplace I found infectious. I bought the book, read it avidly, and resolved to follow the lovely Windrush myself one day. In the meantime, Margaret and I would content ourselves by 'doing a Macarthur' on our own little river, the Amber.

But whereas the London-based Macarthurs - complete with tent and provisions - arrived at the source of their chosen river on foot, after alighting from their train at the nearest station, our journey would need to be made on a day-to-day basis, spread over several weeks. And while Macarthur had his wife by his side to jog his memory and offer support generally as he recorded the day's events by the evening camp fire, Margaret and I had to return to our separate homes at the end of each day, leaving me to record what I could at the kitchen table, amending my notes, if need be, later.

This was a far from ideal arrangement but I could see no alternative. Margaret, however, had other ideas. Why not make use of her stenography skills and record my impressions as we went along? She could then provide me with these in written form later, and together with my end-of-day notes, they should provide sufficient detail for me to write a full account of our explorations.

And so, one Sunday morning in April, we alighted from the bus at a windswept crossroads to the south of Beeley Moor, between Matlock and Chesterfield, to begin our search for the source of the Amber. According to our map, there were two claimants for this distinction, about a mile apart, neither of which was accessible by public footpath. Macarthur, I recalled, had paid little heed to such niceties, clambering over walls and forcing his way through clumps of bushes in pursuit of his objective, on one occasion relying on his wife's charms to placate a potentially-obstructive farmer with wide-eyed questions about Gloucestershire's cricketing giant, Wally Hammond.

Despite the fact that our map showed a feature called Gladwin's Mark nearby, I could hardly expect Margaret to employ a similar tactic by confronting an indignant landowner with a similar approach concerning the Derbyshire bowler of that name. Instead, we opted for a conveniently-situated footpath midway between the two; after all, we convinced ourselves, we could always return later to track down the actual source.

Beyond the hamlet of Uppertown, another footpath brought us to the confluence of the two streams that had begun a mile apart. We rejoiced. We now had a real river to follow. Margaret's shorthand skills were soon fully employed, recording my every impression. Alas, all too soon, footpath and river went their separate ways; we into the village of Kelstedge, the Amber plunging beneath the busy Chesterfield-to-Matlock road at the foot of Slack Hill. Soon, however, we were on familiar ground, entering Ashover - a favourite village of ours - below which the Amber, a fully-fledged river by now, and marked as such on our map, had a delightful scenic footpath for company as far as Milltown, from which we had to return to Ashover to catch the bus home.

It took three more day-walks to complete our journey along the River to its confluence with the Derwent at Ambergate. Enjoyable though these walks were, I knew in my heart on their completion that I had nowhere near enough material to write a book, even supposing I had the faintest idea of how to get it published in the first place. Mrs Fairbrother, whom I had consulted throughout, and who had been dismissive of the whole idea from the outset, was brutally, if characteristically frank.

'Journalism and authorship are two entirely different things,' she reminded me. 'I must say, you seem to have lost sight of why you took your journalism course. Writing books may come later. But first, you must get a foot on the ladder, and that means reporting. It won't pay much part-time but it'll be a start. Go and see the man at the local weekly's office.' Clearly she detected my lack of enthusiasm at the suggestion. 'You won't be down the pit for ever – at least I hope not,' she added in slightly softer tones. 'Reporting – the routine stuff – may be dull, but remember, all the top-notch reporters started that way.'

I could have predicted how the homily would end. 'Don't forget – always aim high!'

\*\*\*\*\*\*\*\*\*\*\*\*\*\*\*\*\*

Mr Plumtree looked up at me with a mixture of curiosity and amusement. 'Mine's a one-man band,' he explained. 'I had an assistant at one time but he left to better himself pay-wise. Can't say that I blame him.' He stroked his chin reflectively. 'Yes, I suppose I  could use a part-timer – on a lineage basis, of course, depending on, well  -  writing ability and availability for evening work.' I informed him that I already contributed a weekly nature notes column to the paper, and added that I was involved in amateur dramatics. Evening work, I assured him, was exactly what I was looking for, to begin with at least.

Mr Plumtree pondered. Hmm, help with evening events - reporting plays especially - would be most welcome. He rummaged among the clutter on his desk and produced a notebook and pencil. Perhaps if he took my phone number? I gulped in dismay. We weren't on the phone, I explained, with as much dignity as I could muster. Mr Plumtree raised an eyebrow, noted my address instead, and offered me his card. I would need to ring him regularly for assignments, he reminded me. Oh, and what about transport? He was a motorbike man himself. Did I - ?   I cycled, I mumbled, or travelled by bus. I detected a dubious pout of the lips.

'Well, let's see how you get on, anyway,' he said.  'Oh,

and you'll need this.' He produced a card marked 'Press' with a safety pin attached. 'Don't forget to print your name on it. You'll need to show it at plays and suchlike. Otherwise you'll have to pay to get in.'

I thanked him and turned to go. 'Just a minute – here's the very thing for your first job.' He produced a complimentary ticket for a play being staged in a nearby village during the following week. 'Be sure to turn up on the opening night,' Mr Plumtree advised, adding with a grin. 'They like to read how good they are before the show ends. They may not be up to West End standard but they love to see their names in print.'

The implication of the reporter's words began to sink in at last. The play, like those in which I took part, ran for four nights. I would need to write my report immediately after the first performance and post it next morning. Mr Plumtree had anticipated the question taking shape in my mind. 'You'll need to send your report straight to head office,' he informed me. 'Do your best – they'll knock it into shape. In fact you'll hardly recognise it by the time they've finished with it.'

My mind was in turmoil as I rode home. Somehow the bottom rung of the ladder into journalism was almost within reach, and yet....... How could I possibly become a drama critic overnight? The very idea was preposterous. And what would my parents say, they who regarded newspaper reporters, if not with out-and-out contempt, then certainly with deep mistrust? Well at least, whatever I wrote would appear in print anonymously.

To my relief, my news was received with a calmness bordering on indifference, possibly because I gave only the sketchiest outline of what was entailed. Mrs Fairbrother, by contrast, was delighted.

'Excellent – just the start you need!' she enthused. 'And don't just restrict yourself to reporting plays. Go out looking for stories – they're there, waiting to be discovered.' She grimaced. 'You can't possibly do worse than the rubbish they print every week. The paper needs new ideas. Show them what you can do!' After confessing my apprehension at tackling my first play report, Mrs Fairbrother produced several back issues of the paper. 'I keep these for lighting the fires,' she explained. 'That's all they're good enough for.' A search revealed a few reports of past productions – the work, she presumed, of Mr Plumtree. The grimace returned as she read out extracts:

'A memorable evening's entertainment. A rip-roaring performance. A laugh from beginning to end. The cast had the audience eating out of their hands.' Snorting with contempt, she thrust the papers towards me. 'Such rot! What does he know about acting? Never stepped on a stage in his life, likely as not. You can do better than that – if you can't, heaven help you!'

The old lady's faith was touching, I reflected as I made my way home, clutching the papers. But justifying it was another matter entirely.

# Chapter 32

With my 'Press' card pinned carefully to my lapel, I presented myself at the ticket table in the doorway of the village hall in which the play was about to begin its four-night run. Flattered, I was ushered to a seat at the front, given a programme and wished an enjoyable evening.

Which, in normal circumstances, perhaps it might have been. But while the rest of the audience were able to sit back and revel in the antics being enacted on stage, I found myself wrestling with a problem; how I could possibly describe in acceptable terms the willing, yet woefully amateur rendering of this run-of-the-mill comedy without resorting to the cliché-ridden style of Mr Plumtree, so scathingly dismissed by Mrs Fairbrother?

Late - much later - that evening, brooding over my typewriter, I was forced to face up to reality. I couldn't. My report, laboured over, re-written countless times and finally typed with weary resignation, came over, to me at least, as ponderous, patronising and predictable. In short, it would have done Mr Plumtree proud.

Opening the paper in trepidation, I discovered that my account had been printed word for word, alongside a curtain-call photograph of the beaming cast, and under a headline entirely in keeping with my lacklustre text. Mr Plumtree, when I rang concerning future assignments, was enthusiastic. I'd got off to a good start, he declared, and with the autumn play season now under way, he could confidently offer me more opportunities, so if I had my diary ready.......

And so, somewhat reluctantly, I found myself increasingly committed to evening work. And while the financial rewards, though meagre, were welcome, these demands, coupled with the day's work underground, began to take their toll. I had already had to forego a part in my own dramatic society's autumn production and unwisely allowed Mr Plumtree to persuade me to cover it for the paper. I was received rather coolly at the first night's performance and made to understand in no uncertain way that I had crossed a real if invisible divide, which a favourable write-up would do little to bridge.

Worse was to follow. The drama section of the newly-formed local arts society chose a contemporary work by a controversial playwright as their opening production and my admittedly sketchy understanding of its theme, as revealed in my report, led to strident protests, causing me considerable embarrassment. Mr Plumtree, however, treated the matter dismissively.

'You're bound to tread on a few toes, sooner or later, in this game,' he reassured me. 'It'll all be forgotten by next week.' He chuckled. 'Serves them right for dishing up highfalutin' stuff like that. I don't suppose anybody in the audience understood it either, even if they pretended to.'

Mrs Fairbrother, too, dismissed my concern with characteristic forthrightness. 'I must say, you'll have to develop a thicker skin,' she asserted. 'Take a leaf out of your father's book and say fie! to the lot of them! You've got your future to think about – surely you're not going to let a few would-be intellectuals put you off?' She went on to remind me of all the other writing opportunities awaiting me; she'd heard, for instance, of the impending retirement of a colliery official in a nearby village - a neighbour of her niece and something of a colourful character; surely he'd have a worthwhile tale or two to tell......... Well, what was I waiting for?

During the months that followed, I did my utmost to develop the 'nose-for-news' advocated in my journalism course and endorsed by Mrs Fairbrother. I bombarded the paper with reports of interviews, events, road accidents and snippets of every imaginable kind, some of which appeared in their entirety; others were edited out of all recognition; while yet others – and chiefly those I considered the most interesting – disappeared without trace.

Meanwhile, I devoted what little time and energy that remained to pursuing my principal aim of researching and writing on countryside topics, which, though clearly incapable of earning me a living, at least fulfilled a deep-seated need to produce work of a more satisfying kind. With the passing of time, however, the question of how best to prepare for the future took on an ever-increasing urgency; what guarantee, if any, was there that this spray-shot approach to writing would secure me a job as a journalist when I was free to leave the mines? Come to that – and leaving aside Mrs Fairbrother's allusions to the giddy heights attained by the best reporters – was I absolutely certain that I wanted a career in the fourth estate anyway?

I decided to confront Mr Plumtree with the burning question head-on. What were my chances of becoming a full-time reporter in, say, three years' time? Mr Plumtree was wary. For once, there was no twinkle of the eye, scarcely a raised eyebrow even; the pause, the tightening of the facial muscles – were ominous. What was to follow confirmed my worst suspicions.

The best journalists – those whose names adorned the national dailies – were weaned on printer's ink, Mr Plumtree said. They had started young, as cub reporters, had quickly found their feet, and had single-mindedly set about ascending the ladder to the big time. Many had failed in the upward struggle, to end up languishing in the backwaters of provincial journalism, there to remain. It was a hard life in a pitiless world and those that withstood the pace and gained the laurels deserved their success.

He, Stan Plumtree, had come into journalism almost by chance. A shop assistant before war service, he had tried insurance after being demobbed, only to find plodding the streets and foot-in-the-door salesmanship something of a dead end.

'Which is what this job is, come to that,' he confessed with a mirthless chuckle. 'I've got as far as I'm going to get and it's no good pretending otherwise. It's a living, that's all I can say for it. But as for career opportunities for a young chap in your position, well.......'

He left the rest unsaid. I thanked him. At least I knew where I stood as far as a career in journalism was concerned.

*****************

I hit rock-bottom that winter. My prospects seemed hopeless. I had wasted my parents' money on a journalism course and a typewriter and all I had to show for it were a few articles and a few pounds in the savings bank. Worse still, I hadn't the faintest idea what other career opportunities, if any, were open to me. In three years' time, I would be free to leave the mines – but then what? With each passing day, the often-quoted saw, 'Once a miner, always a miner', seemed to become an ever-closer reality, a destiny that I had no means of escaping, and one the very contemplation of which filled me with bitter despair.

Who could I turn to? Clearly my parents - bewildered at the way in which their one and only offspring had somehow got into this unhappy state - were powerless to help. Margaret, willing as ever but herself confined within the bounds of a conventional working-class background, was in no position to suggest what to do. And although Mrs Fairbrother remained the obvious person in whom to confide, I found myself unable to face her with the news of my shattered hopes over journalism and instead made a point of avoiding her. There seemed to be no way out. Why not resign myself to my fate?

Which for a time, I did. At work, I put on an act I intended to be seen as worldly cynicism. I even made a point of restricting my work to a bare minimum, only to panic and attempt frantically to catch up on the backlog when my negligence seemed in danger of being exposed.

Despite my efforts to the contrary however, this self-deception began to affect my private life. Black moods, though little more than sulks at first, increased both in frequency and severity until my relationship with the long-suffering Margaret was put under almost impossible strain and saved only by her yielding to my abject pleas for forgiveness when the gloom clouds finally lifted.

Thankfully, the coming of spring brought some relief. I resumed my after-work bike rides, feeding my senses hungrily on the greening hedges, the flower-spangled banks, and as ever, the birds that adorned them. Occasionally I passed a ruddy-faced farm worker labouring in the fields or driving a herd of cattle at a leisurely pace along a lane. Could this kind of work offer a solution? After all, one branch of Mother's family had been farmers, apparently contented with their lot and living to a ripe old age. Farming had changed dramatically in recent times but it remained an open-air life, closer than any other to mother earth. Maybe this was to be my destiny after all.

One afternoon, having resolved to write an article on a nearby village, I set off to photograph the church. Afterwards, descending the churchyard steps, I was confronted by a group of young children, just emerged from the nearby school. We exchanged friendly greetings and I was about to ride off when one of the group, a stocky-built lad in a shabby raincoat and wellingtons, his face beaming, pointed to my camera.

'Ey up, mister, tek our photo.'

Within seconds, he had assembled a motley little group, boys and girls, in front of the steps and taking his place in the line, grinning widely, informed me that they were ready. The picture taken, the group dispersed, chattering excitedly and I headed for home, unaware that the incident was to have a significant bearing on my future life.

# Chapter 33

Father made sure that Mother was out of earshot before raising the subject. 'Mrs Fairbrother called to me over the fence this morning. She says she can't understand why you haven't been round lately.'

I tried evasion, though without success. I was twenty-three but that had little bearing on the matter. He'd dropped a hint and in case that proved insufficient he added for emphasis 'Just make sure you get round there before very long, that's all.'

Inwardly I knew I couldn't keep on avoiding the old lady indefinitely so I decided I'd best get it over with, and the sooner the better. She'd have to know about Mr Plumtree's verdict eventually but if I could get her to discuss plans for future articles it would hopefully soften her reaction. I thought I'd take the latest batch of photographic prints as evidence that I had not abandoned writing completely. Anything to avoid a lengthy inquest on the end of my brief career as a journalist.

Mrs Fairbrother had a visitor. Following her into the spacious drawing room, I recognised her niece, a young married woman who taught in a nearby school, and with whom I'd chatted briefly over the years. Like me, she was evidently prepared to exchange pleasantries. Not so her aunt.

'Of course, you've met my neighbour's son,' she began with her customary briskness. 'He's the young man who's frittering away his life down the pit when he's capable of so much more.' Squirming with embarrassment, I attempted to explain the reason for my intrusion but Mrs Fairbrother swept it aside. 'His father tells me that he's been advised that he's too old to make a career in journalism, even though he writes well.' So she knew! Father had put her in the picture already; I breathed an inward sigh of relief.

Anxious to demonstrate my determination to continue

with my writing, I produced the photographs, commenting on each as I passed them to the two women, seated side by side on the settee. On reaching the group of smiling children, I saw an opportunity to lighten the atmosphere by describing how the photograph came to be taken. Mrs Fairbrother's niece looked up.

'You obviously get on well with children,' she observed. 'Have you ever thought of becoming a teacher?'

I was dumbstruck. The idea had never so much as crossed my mind. I knew no teachers. They inhabited a different world from mine. True, I had encountered a couple during my amateur dramatic society days and had been in awe of their confident, sophisticated manner, but as for becoming a teacher myself..........

Mrs Fairbrother was quick to take up the subject. 'Yes – why not? They're crying out for teachers. Isn't that true, Sonia?' She gave one of her contemptuous snorts. 'Different from my day, I must say. Teaching posts were like gold dust then.'

While the two women discussed the changing times in the profession, I tried to marshal my jumbled thoughts into some kind of order. Despite my abysmal exam results all those years ago, was it possible, even now, to make amends? Surely that was too much to hope for? And yet, perhaps...... .

'Of course, it would mean more studying,' Mrs Fairbrother resumed her theme with renewed vigour. 'You'd need to improve your School Certificate and add a few subjects at advanced level to qualify for a place at training college. But you've more than two years in which to do it.'

I was conscious of two pairs of eyes searching my face, awaiting my response. I needed time to think – or was it merely to delay making a decision? Did I really want to demonstrate the truth of 'Once a miner, always a miner'? Or could farm work, or any other manual labour, fulfil my needs?

Mrs Fairbrother's niece - less strident than her aunt, yet equally forceful - came to my rescue. 'I'll find out how you can obtain details of late-entry procedure,' she promised. 'Then at least you'll know what's entailed.'

The last word, inevitably, was Mrs Fairbrother's. 'This could be the biggest decision you've ever made,' she pronounced. 'What you do in the next two years will determine your future – simple as that.'

****************

The man at the local education office was sympathetic, though cautious. Yes, there were indeed places in training colleges for mature students; in fact, such late entrants to the profession were on the whole a better long-term investment than younger students. However, he felt he must stress that to secure a place in two years' time I would need to upgrade my modest School Certificate. The obvious way to do this would be by attending evening classes in Derby, commencing in the autumn. I realised, he assumed, that in addition to attendance at classes, I would need to allow time for homework and private study? In other words, if I was to ensure acceptance as a trainee teacher, I would need to devote virtually the whole of my leisure time over the next two years to achieving that aim. He trusted he had made himself perfectly clear?

I assured him that he had and stepped outside into the springtime promise of a late afternoon with a renewed sense of purpose.

****************

But first there was our holiday. Ever since devouring Wilson Macarthur's book on the River Windrush, I had set my heart on visiting the Cotswolds and now at last this ambition was about to be realised. Margaret and I had arranged to spend the second of our two weeks' leave entitlement cycling in the region and so, having booked ourselves accommodation in a cottage overlooking a spacious green in a village on the Warwickshire-Oxfordshire border, we cycled to Derby station, put our bikes in the guard's van, and took our seats for the journey to Banbury.

There followed a week of sheer delight, seeing for ourselves views and villages glimpsed hitherto only in the sepia-toned pages of books. Ill-versed in the complexities of where to stay in such an extensive area, we had chosen a base out on the north-eastern limits of the Cotswolds, thus confining ourselves to places within comfortable cycling distance of our cottage near Shipston-on-Stour. Consequently, we never quite managed to reach the valley of the River Windrush, being utterly absorbed in exploring a host of delectable places all around us, while at the same time promising ourselves a return visit to sample more distant delights later.

The week was made even more enjoyable by the turn of events at home. With my mind now set exclusively on qualifying for teacher- training, I no longer entertained fanciful hopes of writing about our discoveries. And so, freed from such self-imposed obligations, I was able to enjoy the brief holiday for its own sake. Not that this freedom extended to our personal relationship; as on previous holidays, and despite the free-and-easy attitude of our hostess - a cheerful, cherubic widow, who let it be known that she made a habit of settling in front of her newly-acquired television set until close-down - intimacy ended with a goodnight kiss at Margaret's bedroom door.

A faded collection of black and white photographs bears testimony to our endeavours to fill every moment with new discoveries during that precious week. Each day's route was planned with our customary precision and calculated to encompass every attainable feature of the landscape deemed unmissable in my well-thumbed guide books. The week saw us gazing in awe at the splendid Tudor pile of Compton Wynyates; captivated by the chocolate-box charm of Great Tew and earnestly seeking out venerable old churches in a string of quaint ginger-biscuit-coloured ironstone villages.

One day, having savoured the remoteness of Little Rollright, we made our way to the celebrated Stones, only too willing to succumb to their powerful mysticism. And although their setting - to our eyes at least - failed to compare with that of our own familiar Arborlow, here were standing stones in plenty - not merely a circle, but with others huddled in a conspiratorial group some way down the hillside, strange and sinister. Alone on this sweep of upland, where Warwickshire and Oxfordshire met, the tales we had read about this prehistoric monument took on a new reality. We found ourselves speaking in whispers, as though not wishing to disturb – we knew not what.

On our final day, we made for Broadway, a place that we had been led to believe epitomised the very best in Cotswold villages. Who could fail to be impressed by the stage-set perfection of the place? And yet, pushing our bikes past the immaculately- maintained buildings of golden stone, avoiding the luxurious cars unloading sleekly-dressed guests outside sumptuous hotels, it was with mixed feelings that we headed for Fish Hill, to climb the escarpment before cruising down into Chipping Campden.

Here, by contrast, true perfection awaited us – a little town, ancient and venerable, yet lacking any trace of the smugness and sophistication we had sensed at Broadway. We lingered long on the exquisite High Street, feasting our senses on the timeless beauty of the Market Hall, the Woolstaplers' Hall, Grevel House and a host of other noble buildings, before moving on to admire the almshouses, the gatehouse to Sir Baptist Hicks' ill-fated mansion, and St James' church, with its glorious tower commanding the landscape for miles around.

Cycling back to our lodgings, tired but richly fulfilled after a day packed with memorable experiences, we passed two young boys playing by the roadside. Looking up at our approach, they watched us pass in silence before one called after us in broad Cotswold: 'Carrn't you go any farrster than tharrt?'

Laughing, we continued on our way, attempting from time to time to imitate, with varying degrees of success, the unfamiliar dialect. Soon - all too soon - this light-hearted incident, together with all the other happenings that delighted us on our brief holiday, would  be but a memory as the urgency of daily life laid claim to us once more.

# Chapter 34

That September I enrolled for three evening classes – in geography, biology and English literature. The first two were held in the technical college, whereas the literature class took place in the annexe of a severe Victorian grammar school building some distance away. To begin with, I cycled the twelve miles each way, enjoying the ride into Derby in the cool of late autumn afternoons and relishing equally the homeward pedal, with its chance to reflect on the evening's lesson.

With the onset of winter, however, I travelled by bus, which enabled me to study on the way. There were times though, when after a particularly strenuous day's work, I found the gentle vibration of the homeward journey had a soothing effect and I had to fight against sleep to avoid missing my stop. Occasionally, the demands of work meant that I was late arriving home on evening-class days and this meant a frantic rush to catch my bus. I had decided from the start that I would keep news of my resumption of studying from the other survey staff, for although I felt sure that Tim Woolley would not have made life difficult for me, I knew that the same could not be said for certain others.

Fortunately for me, Tim had married recently and whereas in the past he had often preferred to carry out special surveys on the night shift, it was noticeable that he no longer favoured that option, otherwise I would have had to miss some of my classes.

Despite the travelling and the inevitable tiredness, I found the classes stimulating and enjoyable. Thanks to the journalism course and the local history classes I had recently attended, I adjusted readily enough to studying and with an objective now clear within my sights, I had all the motivation I needed.

Of my three chosen subjects, biology was by far the easiest. A good deal of the coursework had changed little from that of my distant schooldays, while my knowledge of natural history was a distinct advantage. As it happened, the lecturer, an animated youngish woman with a lively teaching style, had read my articles in the county magazine. After making the connection and learning of my circumstances, she proffered valuable advice on teaching generally and in so doing gave my self-confidence a welcome boost.

The geography class was a large one, in which I seemed to be one of the oldest members. I struck up a friendship of sorts with a lean, wild-eyed youth, desperately unhappy with his stifling office job, who made a habit of arriving early and beckoning me over to the next desk. He had recently discovered the writings of Richard Jefferies, and was especially excited about the Wiltshire-born nature writer's autobiographical *The Story of My Heart*. Having, like me, squandered his schooldays opportunities, he was trying desperately to make amends, though seemingly without much idea of what he wanted to do with his life once he had broken free from his sterile desk-bound routine. A townsman through and through, he ranted excitedly about his search for Jefferies' 'Soul life', without, it seemed, having an inkling of the intense intimacy with the natural world upon which his hero's philosophy was based.

The geography lecturer – dapper, bow-tied, his bald crown flanked by tufts of unruly hair - missed no opportunity to air his caustic wit, reserving his keenest barbs for late-comers, militant feminists and global capitalism. There was no denying his mastery of his subject, however, and I found myself relishing his colourful, provocative lectures.

A complete contrast was provided by the elderly, donnish teacher who conducted the English literature class. Silver-haired, with spectacles lodged permanently mid-way between bridge and nose-tip, his sober, not-quite-shabby appearance was perfectly in keeping with the sombre gothic building in which the class was held. What really mattered, of course, was the quality of his teaching, and once again I had struck lucky. For here was a man whose enthusiasm for language and literature – be it Shakespeare, Wells, or the Victorian poets – was positively infectious, to me at least, and provided the perfect incentive to get to grips with fine writing, not merely to satisfy an examiner but for sheer personal pleasure.

\*\*\*\*\*\*\*\*\*\*\*\*\*\*\*\*\*

With three evenings of the week devoted to my classes, it meant that virtually all of my remaining spare time was taken up with writing essays and in study generally. This was no hardship during the winter months but with the approach of spring, I yearned to get out into the open air. Weather permitting, we still treated ourselves to a weekend ramble or cycle ride and occasionally I snatched a precious hour or so out of doors after work. But as I had set myself the target of achieving good results in the June examinations before applying to enter training college, there was no alternative but to drive myself hard.

Mrs. Fairbrother, meanwhile, continued to take a lively interest in my doings. Providing that I obtained the necessary qualifications to enter college, she assured me, the rest would be straightforward. In her eyes, the teaching profession, like the world of newspapers, was comprised largely of lacklustre and incompetent individuals; after two years' training, she insisted, local education authorities throughout the land would be vying for my services.

'You'll sail through!' she declared. 'Get that two years at college out of the way and there'll be no holding you!

Remember – aim high! Go for promotion –don't linger with the also-rans. From what my niece tells me, most of the men teachers are much like they were in my day – tweedy, weedy or seedy. Show them what you're made of!'

I wondered how on earth I could live up to such high expectations and attempted to change the subject, implying that my writing career looked set to end now that I intended becoming a teacher.

'Nonsense!' came the reply. 'Keep up your writing – and expand it. I must say, the educational press is badly in need of new talent, from what I hear. Get busy with that typewriter of yours!'

But first I had to put everything into the crucial exams. That spring, our evening walks were confined to short strolls as far as a grassy bank close to the village, where we would settle down and Margaret would proceed to test me on some aspect of my studies from my notes and textbooks. I'd also entered certain facts, quotations and other information in a small notebook which I carried around with me at work, taking furtive peeps from time to time with the light of my lamp. I found that I could put the time spent on long walks underground to good use by repeating to myself extracts and quotes from my literature set books – an exercise which helped to relieve the monotony of plodding through the darkness in the company of a silent and often sullen workmate.

As the time for the exams drew near, I realised that I would need to ask Tim Woolley for permission to take part of my two weeks' annual leave in odd days. This would mean revealing the nature of my future plans, for if all went well I should require more time off later to attend for interview at training college. Tim expressed surprise at my news but agreed readily enough to my request; however, the inevitable consequence was that in no time my intentions were common knowledge both in the survey office and at the colliery and I was subjected to a fair amount of ribbing. Most of this, down the pit especially, was good-natured. One old man never tired of repeating the age-old saying: 'Yoh can allus tell a skewl teycher – but yoh canna tell 'im much.' Another made a point of warning me against becoming 'stuck up' in my new career, while yet another questioned whether I knew enough to be able to impart any worthwhile knowledge to my future pupils.

I was also regaled with countless stories concerning the men's own schooldays. Most of these memories related to misdemeanours committed and punishments received, which without exception were severe in the extreme. The schoolmasters responsible came over as sadists of the most brutal kind and yet more often than not the teller of the tale would conclude his narrative with 'I 'ad many a thrashin' but it did me no 'arm', or 'We were frit to death o' 'im but 'e were a damn good teycher.' I lost count of the times I was asked if I'd started practising with my cane – somewhat premature, for as I was at pains to point out, I had yet to obtain a place in training college.

# Chapter 35

The wait for the results seemed interminable. I had felt reasonably confident with my performance at the time but the nagging little doubts that began to assail me as the weeks passed seemed to multiply to such an extent that by the time August arrived I was beginning to think the unthinkable. What if I had failed? It was vital that I did well in all three subjects, otherwise my future plans would be thrown into disarray. I could not afford to fail. And yet............

And now, after eight years of working underground, with release in sight at last, the strain of it all began to tell. The distant hills looked more enticing than ever as I cycled to work one beautiful summer morning. A busy day lay ahead. It was the last Friday of the month and this meant that, assisted by Neville, I had to measure the amount of progress made by a number of coal faces a considerable distance from the shaft bottom. This entailed several miles of walking, along roadways scarcely five feet high in places due to subsidence, and although the work was straightforward and normally took comparatively little time in itself, the distances we had to travel meant that the shift would be a long one.

I donned my pit clothes and made my way to the lamp room. There had been no sign of Neville in the changing room, indicating that he would be late yet again and have a frantic rush getting to the pit-head in time. I spent a few minutes discussing the county's cricket fortunes with the lamp- room attendant, expecting a breathless Neville to burst in at any moment – in vain. Disconsolately, I set off for the pit-head. There was a slender chance that if he arrived late, the banksman would allow him to descend before coal-winding resumed, as he had done, grudgingly, on previous occasions. I had a word with the man in question and extracted a half-promise. I could only hope.

Tense with frustration, I waited in the pit bottom office for half an hour. Realising by then that there would be no Neville, and all too aware of the demands of the shift ahead, I tried to obtain the services of one of the youths employed on haulage work, only to be told that no-one could be spared. I was left with no alternative but to set off alone.

Working single-handedly was nothing new to me; I had learned to cope on my own with my routine linesman's work over the years and although it entailed a good deal of extra fetching and carrying, in some ways I found it preferable to having to rely on a surly and at times uncooperative assistant. When it came to measuring long distances with a linen tape, however, a second pair of hands was essential. My only hope was that I could enlist the help of someone to hold the end of the tape for me in each of the widely scattered coal faces I had to visit.

To begin with, all went well. I managed to find a deputy or a workman willing to spare a few minutes to lend a hand and by snap-time I estimated that I was not far behind my intended schedule. So far so good. As the day proceeded, however, predictable delays occurred. On one face I had to wait while shot-firing operations took place. On another, a tub derailment had resulted in pit props being scattered all over the roadway. In each case, no help was forthcoming and the only way I could carry out my task was by weighting the end of the tape under a heavy object and trudging to and fro to release it.

By now, it was well into the afternoon and wearily plodding my way towards the last and most distant face, I met the colliers who worked there on their way back to the pit bottom at the end of their shift. As the faint glow of their lamps faded into the darkness, it dawned on me that until the afternoon shift deputy arrived, I would be entirely alone in this labyrinth of workings, two miles from the pit bottom.

And now, for the very first time in all these years, an overpowering uneasiness gripped me. A combination of anger, despair and worst of all, fear, it pulled me up in my tracks. Clammy sweat made my skin creep; I could neither go on nor turn back. Suddenly, something snapped inside. Pent-up emotions - held back for too long - burst free in an uncontrollable torrent. As though detached from it all, I heard my bitter sobs and raging curses shatter the silence. Self-loathing overwhelmed me. Why, I heard myself scream, had I allowed my parents to dictate how I should live my life? Why, when I could have served two years of national service and been free to choose a worthwhile career, had I wasted all these years scrabbling around in dirt and darkness? What if, now that my sentence was almost served, I fell victim to injury – death even – such as the fate that befell so many in this godforsaken calling? And how on earth could I face my parents, Margaret, Mrs Fairbrother, my workmates – if I failed my exams? Above all, how could I face myself?

Later – some time later – I became aware of an inner calm. Emotionally drained, I sensed nevertheless that an immense burden had been lifted from my spirits and that I had overcome - for the time being at least – whatever dark force had lurked within my mind. It was time to complete the job I had set out to do.

The coal face, when at last I reached it, was deserted, as I knew it would be. As before, I set about the laborious task of measuring by anchoring the end of the tape with lumps of rock and trudging back and forth to calculate the distance progressed. From time to time as I worked, the absolute silence was broken by the distant rumble of a roof fall in the worked-out seam on either side or by the trickle of rock particles from the roof above. A residue of uneasiness lingered and I knew that I had to stifle it before it reasserted itself. I recalled that, as a child, I had dared myself to approach the nearby wood at dusk. I had shouted my defiance into the darkness, boasting of the array of weaponry I carried. Now, rather than resorting to the adult equivalent – whistling in the dark - I turned to Shakespeare, quoting aloud speeches from *Richard II* that I had memorized for the English literature exam. The absurdity of this was not entirely lost on me; never before, surely, had the work of the greatest of dramatists echoed deep in the bowels of the earth, to an audience of pit props and tramway rails.

*****************

Not content with extracting every cobble of deep-mined coal that could be dug from the ring of mines encircling our village, the powers-that-be renewed their efforts to supplement this output by extending opencast working. As a result, a huge excavator, dwarfing the highest buildings for miles around, was assembled uncomfortably close to my home, its superstructure towering over the rooftops. Operating round the clock, its night- lights flashing wildly, this monster - and the ceaseless shuttle of lorries it filled - brought noise, dirt and discomfort to everyone in the village, while at the same time rendering our local footpaths out of bounds as wire fences and 'Keep out' signs spread in a hideous rash across the few remaining fields.

Having been for some time a regular listener to *The Northcountryman*, a weekly radio miscellany programme in which contributors read their own offerings, I decided to put to use some of the time spent awaiting my results in writing about the effects that this vast piece of machinery was having on the village. Reasonably competent at typing by now, I submitted what I hoped was a passable script before turning my attention to other matters. Even if nothing came of it, I reasoned, at least I'd demonstrated to my parents that I was still making use of their expensive gift. I saw it too, as a gesture to Mrs. Fairbrother, whose faith in me had remained steadfast throughout, and whose loathing of the giant excavator was such that given the strength, she would gladly have torn it apart with her bare hands.

The uplifting of my spirits that had followed the outburst underground brought with it a renewed determination, not merely to endure what remained of my time in the pit but to somehow put it to future use, though exactly how I had as yet no idea. Accordingly, I began noting incidents, impressions, modes of speech – anything that struck me as worth recording and that might one day be deserving of recall. And if my worst fear – failure in my exams – proved justified, I would sit them again – and again if necessary. And if a place in training college was denied me, then somehow I would find some other opening. Come to that, I told myself, I'd relish the challenge.

This eventuality did not arise, however. Within days I learned that I had obtained comfortable passes in all three subjects. And next day I received word that my submission to *The Northcountryman* had been accepted and I was invited to Leeds to record it.

# Chapter 36

**B**ut for my steel toe-capped boots, there would have been a distinct spring in my step as I entered my last year as a miner. I wasted no time in getting down to further study, spent an enjoyable day travelling to Leeds to record my talk, and armed with the news of my recent exam successes, paid another visit to the local education office.

The man behind the desk, higher up the seniority ladder, I suspected, than the man I had seen on my previous visit, was both helpful and friendly. He couldn't foresee me having any difficulty in getting into college but obviously evidence of continuing my studies would help. I would need to decide on a preference order of colleges from the national list; bearing in mind my particular interest in the countryside, he would willingly advise me on making this choice. In the meantime he would investigate my entitlement to a grant to cover my two years of training and would also try to secure for me a spell of unqualified teaching in the months between my leaving the pit and entering college.

The following spring and summer, a new interest added spice to our countryside rides and rambles. I had set my heart on teaching junior-age children and I found myself covetously eyeing every village school we passed. It being the weekend, the schools were closed and to get any idea of what went on within it was necessary to peer through windows, read notices pinned to boards and gates and speculate what use, if any, was made of the immediate environment.

I also found myself eavesdropping on conversation between teachers on buses, in shops or in the street. More often than not, the audible fragments I picked up merely confirmed that teachers were ordinary people, preoccupied with humdrum concerns. What could I expect? Unlike me, they had most likely entered college straight from school; had become teachers as a matter of course; and had otherwise given the matter little thought. By contrast, I, having wasted precious years, felt privileged to be given the chance to train for teaching and couldn't wait to enter the profession. In fact, I could hardly contain my delight at the prospect.

That Easter, I was summoned for interview to the first college of my choice. Although on the edge of an ancient west midlands city, it was a comparatively new college, having opened as an emergency training establishment in prefabricated buildings immediately after the war. It stood in the grounds of a former Victorian mansion, now part of the expanding college, and the walled gardens, orchards and paddocks gave it a look of rural permanence that belied its age. It was immediately evident why the man at the education office had strongly recommended it as my first choice. Full advantage had been taken of the site to develop a range of rural and environmental studies; a farm, garden plots and nature trails had been established and with open countryside close at hand, I knew straight away that this was the place for me.

But first, there was the matter of my interview. Together with a dozen or so other potential entrants, male and female, of various ages, I was shown round the empty college. I struck up an acquaintance with a man several years my senior who intended leaving a responsible position in industry to fulfil a long-standing ambition to teach. Unlike me, however, he was free to commence training in the coming September, whereas I still had the best part of another year of my sentence to serve. We wished one another well and hoped we'd meet again.

Completely unaware of the form the interview would take, I was in for a pleasant surprise. I was made to feel relaxed, encouraged to talk freely, and assured that whatever the outcome of my further studies, a place awaited me in the academic year after next. Overjoyed, I strode through the quaint old city streets to the station as though walking on air. Not only could my time as a miner now be measured in months, but a whole new life beckoned. Truly a light shone at the end of the tunnel.

\*\*\*\*\*\*\*\*\*\*\*\*\*\*\*\*

The ribbing to which I had been subjected earlier was as nothing compared with that I was now called upon to face. As before, I had tried unsuccessfully to play down my forthcoming switch from the pit to college but my workmates were having none of it. After all, it wasn't every day that one of their number embarked upon a new and entirely different career and the older men in particular intended exploiting the novelty for all it was worth. Seemingly unaware of the changes that had taken place in schools since their own distant days as pupils, they produced a steady stream of tales, chiefly as before relating to their schoolmasters' dexterity with the cane, but also - in the manner of the master in Goldsmith's *Deserted Village* - bearing testimony to their own particular pedagogue's phenomenal powers of scholarship.

The clear implication of all this reminiscing was that I should have my work cut out to be a worthy follower in such men's footsteps – something of which I was all too well aware, even though inwardly I entertained the hope that I would somehow get by without resorting to the brutality that had been regarded as normal in their day.

Practical advice, too, was readily forthcoming. I was recommended to polish up my tables, and especially my 'guzinters' (2 guzinter 4 twice, etc). I was warned to be vigilant over nits (head lice); shady goings-on in the urinals; and the hazards of detaining alluring young girls in class after school. Above all, concern was expressed about what on earth I would find to keep me occupied when faced with such long holidays.

\*\*\*\*\*\*\*\*\*\*\*\*\*\*\*\*\*

The man at the education office was as good as his word. On learning that I would be free to leave the pit several months before entering college, he arranged for me to visit a large junior school in a nearby village one day after work to meet the head teacher with a view to joining his staff in an unqualified capacity for two terms.

The school - a drab building of blackened bricks set in an arid walled playground - was empty and silent by the time I arrived. After searching in vain along echoing corridors, my footfall eventually attracted the attention of a slightly-built careworn-looking man who introduced himself as the head teacher, proffered a limp hand, and led the way into a cramped and cluttered office.

So - I wanted to gain some teaching experience before entering college? Well, yes, he supposed that could be arranged. However, it would be as well for me to know at the outset that the school was run on traditional lines – two-stream entry, A and B. He would try to enable me to spend some time with each class, starting with the lower juniors, but that would depend on the willingness of the staff. His frown intensified. I must appreciate that not all teachers welcomed......I hastened to say I understood. He seemed relieved. Perhaps I would like to look around?

Later, cycling homeward, I reflected on the mingled impressions just gained. Ushered hurriedly from room to room, I had seen obsessive tidiness and hopeless disorder;

wall displays ranging from the tatty and faded to the tasteful and stimulating; craftwork revealing imaginative scope contrasting with the slavishly imitative. Whatever else I stood to gain, I would certainly encounter a wide range of teaching approaches – and teacher personalities too.

Nothing especially memorable marked my last weeks as a miner. A few self- conscious handshakes were exchanged at the end of my last shift and a few good-natured taunts aimed in my direction. Leaving the baths for the last time, I stuffed my overalls into a bin and in passing, hurled my boots and kneepads on to the spoil heap. My life-saving helmet I decided to keep – for old time's sake. I have it still.

As I cycled out of the pit yard, a youth I knew slightly drew alongside.

'Yoh leavin' terday?'

'Yes.'

'Me an' all. Gunna be a slaughterman – better pay. What are tha' doin'?'

'College – then teaching.'

'Bloody 'ell – rather thee than me. Still, I 'spect it's better than th' pit - owt would be.'

He was off, pedalling furiously, before I could frame an apt reply.

# Postscript

Margaret and I were married on a lovely late-summer day of the kind that heralds, in the subtlest of ways, the approach of autumn. The fine old church – the same that I had been photographing on that afternoon, three years earlier, when I met the group of children – overlooked the countryside we loved.

Two former superiors during my time in the mines, Mr Elliston and Walter Thorne, played important roles on the occasion. The former, happily still active in retirement, took it upon himself to effect introductions and attend to matters behind the scenes generally, while Walter, still a bachelor and destined to remain so, discharged the unaccustomed duties of best man with his usual quiet efficiency.

Our honeymoon destination, reached after a long and complicated train and bus journey, was a tiny village on the edge of the Quantock hills, where we were welcomed and fussed over by a jolly old couple who cackled gleefully in rich rounded Somerset accents. The wife's culinary speciality was huge delicious apple dumplings, the likes of which we had never before encountered nor have met with since. The Quantocks captivated us. Without our bikes, and with only an infrequent bus service, we spent the week rambling, map in hand, through rich beechwoods and over heather-clad slopes, catching fleeting glimpses of red deer and stonechats flicking on sprigs of gorse and feasting our eyes on the gull-strewn restless sea, spread out before us far below our clifftop vantage point.

Two weeks later I would be commencing my training as a teacher. A new and entirely different way of life lay ahead.